the identity of Ulster

the land the language
and the people

by

Ian Adamson

First published by Pretani Press 1982.
638 Springfield Road, Belfast BT12 7DY
Second impression 1985.
Second edition 1987.
Copyright © Ian Adamson 1981.

*"Terrible as an army with banners
Through the dusk of a winter's eve,
Over the Bridge
The thousands tramp*

★   ★   ★

*Terrible as an army with banners,
The legions of labour
The builders of ships,
Tramp thro' the winter eve."*

"The Islandmen" by Richard Valentine Williams (Richard Rowley)

A Nosmada Book
All rights reserved.
Printed in Northern Ireland with trade union labour
by W. & G. Baird Ltd.

Paperback   ISBN 0 948868-04-X
Hardback   ISBN 0 948868-05-8

For my Father and Mother.

Old Long Bridge Belfast about 1835.

Queen's Bridge Belfast about 1921.

iv

Contents

"Let us then never look backward, let us look ever forward. If it is permissible, and even useful and necessary, to turn back to study our past, it is only in order to establish what we have been and must no longer be, what we have believed and thought and must no longer believe or think, what we have done and must do nevermore . . .

Respect for man is the supreme law of humanity, and the great, the real goal of history, its only legitimate objective, is the humanisation and emancipation, the real liberty, the prosperity and happiness of each individual living in society. For, in the final analysis, we must clearly recognise that collective liberty and prosperity exist only in so far as they represent the sum of individual liberties and prosperities."

Mikhail Bakunin, (1814–1876)

"There is no culture of any sort of which it could be asserted that it arose altogether independently and without outside influences. While we were busy working out very thoroughly the 'inner contrasts' between different culture patterns, we lost the ability rightly to value the common features which lie at the foundation of every culture; we can no longer see the forest for the trees. Wherever scientific research has undertaken the investigation of a past cultural epoch, it has come upon the remains of still older cultures or of blendings and transfers which plainly reveal the invigorating influence of earlier social patterns."

Rudolf Rocker, *Nationalism and Culture*, 1947

"From now on, men will have to make history by fighting History itself, because History has become the last ontological earthwork of power, the last con by which it hides, behind the promise of a long weekend, its will to endure until the Saturday which will never come."

Raoul Vaneigem, *The Revolution of Everyday Life*, 1972

Acknowledgements

The author is grateful to the Ulster Museum, the Ulster Folk and Transport Museum, the Belfast Central Library, The Sirocco Engineering Works and Mrs. Susan Chicken for permission to reproduce photographs and prints under their copyright. He also extends his thanks to Jackie Hewitt of the Farset Youth Project, Michael Hall, Mary Cummings, Sally Taylor, Linda Ballard and the staff of the Ulster Folk and Transport Museum, the staffs of the Ulster Museum, the Linenhall Library, the Public Records Office of Northern Ireland, the Fort Wayne and Allen County Public Library, Indiana and the Library of Congress, Washington, D.C. He fully appreciates all the help given by friends and scholars alike although their opinions are not necessarily those held by the author. Special thanks are extended to Ken and Anne for the front cover design; to Anne Johnston for the cartography; to Jim Patton for invaluable help with the photographic section and to Margaret Allen, Ann Brown, Vera Govan and Andrea Reid for their care and patience in typing and retyping the manuscript. The author would also like to thank Agnes and Andy: Violet; his grandmother, Isabel (née Sloan) Kerr along with the rest of the family for their love and encouragement through difficult days; George Lyons for expert advice on the transport photographs; Jim Fitzpatrick for permission to use the *Cruithne* artwork. Also included in the book are examples of the work of the author's friends, David McFerran and John Middleton.

SCOTLAND

Glasgow
Edinburgh
AYR

UNITED

LONDONDERRY ANTRIM
TYRONE   WIGTON KIRKCUDBRIGHT   Newcastle
FERMANAGH ARMAGH   Belfast
DOWN
ULSTER   MAN
(NORTHERN
IRELAND)
Leeds   Hull
EIRE   Liverpool
(REPUBLIC OF   Manchester   Sheffield
IRELAND)   Dublin

KINGDOM

WALES

IRELAND   Birmingham

Cardiff   Bristol
London

ENGLAND

O Miles   100

GREAT BRITAIN

THE BRITISH ISLES APPROXIMATELY 1950 A.D. SHOWING THE FIVE NATIONS

Introduction

A Tale of Two Irelands

Set as Ulster is at the North Eastern corner of Ireland, facing Britain across a narrow sea and separated from the rest of Ireland by a zone of little hills known as Drumlins, the characteristics of her language and people have been moulded by movements, large and small, between the two islands since the dawn of human history. P. L. Henry has described the difference between Ulster and the rest of Ireland as: "One of the most deeply rooted, ancient, and from a literary point of view, most productive facts of early Irish History." Furthermore, "Ulster's bond with Scotland counterbalances her lax tie with the rest of Ireland. To say, once more, that this applies only to modern times and to dialects of English would be to miscalculate grossly. Here too the mould was fixed in ancient times and modern developments continue ancient associations. We need but think of the Pictish Kingdoms in both areas, of the Ulster-Scottish Kingdom of Dalriada from the last quarter of the 5th to the close of the 8th century, of the Scottish Kingdom founded under Gaelic leadership in 842, of Irish relations with the Kingdom of the Hebrides and Argyll from the 12th century, particularly the immigration of Hebridean soldiers (gallowglasses) from the 13th to the 16th century. The Gaelic form of this word, Galloglaigh, (i.e. Gallagher) occurs as a family name in Northern Ireland. There was a constant coming and going between North East Ireland and Western Scotland. The Glens of Antrim were in the hands of Scottish Macdonalds by 1400, and for the next two hundred years Gaelic-speaking Scots came in large numbers. The 17th century immigration of a numerous Scots element need not be considered outside the preceding series. It has brought for example Presbyterian Scots with names as familiar on this side as McMenemin and Kennedy, who must be considered rather in the light of homing birds."[1]

The main characteristics of the Ulster people are therefore shared by the people of the rest of Ireland and Western Scotland, areas which have formed with the Isle of Man a Scots-Irish cultural province, "Scottish" in its original sense having meant "Irish". These characteristics are known as "Irishness", while the inhabitants of the cultural Scots-Irish province can be said to possess or have possessed an "Irish nationality". These are both facets of a more enduring ancient British personality obscured by modern English and Irish nationalisms. "Irishness" has been described by Estyn Evans as including "a respect for the past, an indifference to present time, a sense of the unseen world, intellectual curiosity, the gift of poetic imagination, a cynical sense of humour, a brooding melancholy, a subtle conception of what constitutes truth, an ingenious casuistry and a deviousness which are perhaps related to historical experience, and above all, an inexhaustible interest in words, in people and in spiritual matters".[2] The latter has often led to sacerdotalism.

In several ways the Protestants of Ulster exhibit these characteristics as strongly as, if not more strongly than, their Roman Catholic counterparts, so that Ulster remains, as she always has been, the most "Irish" territory in the island of Ireland. Yet, while many of them will admit to Irishness and Irish nationality, the Protestants of Ulster are set firmly against Irish Nationalism. It is often forgotten today that towards the end of the 18th century Belfast Protestants first promoted the idea of an insular Irish nation to unite all classes and creeds while fully supporting Catholic emancipation and attempting to revive the ancient music and literature of Ireland. However, following Daniel O'Connell's campaign for a "Catholic parliament for a Catholic people" Irish Nationalism became identified with Catholic nationalism ("Rome Rule"). By the middle of the 19th century writers of Romantic fiction incorporated the ideal into Medieval Gaelic Ireland, and fostered the mythology of Gaelic patriotic racialism in a new Gaelic nationalism.

The marriage of Catholic and Gaelic nationalisms created suspicion and then hostility among many Protestants towards what was an important part of *their* heritage. Furthermore the blending of Catholic and "Celtic" mysticism helped to create the myth of the blood sacrifice, not only in the minds of the bourgeois nationalists like Patrick Pearse but also of socialists like James Connolly, who was thus unable to identify with the Ulster viewpoint. At the same time there had developed in Ulster a real pride in belonging to an expanding British Empire and later Commonwealth. This feeling was reinforced by the presence of large Ulster communities in Australia, Canada, New Zealand and Southern Africa.

Belfast, the only major port in the British Isles to have forbidden the entry of slave-trading vessels, had become an important industrial centre, with trading outlets throughout the world. This experience of primary industrial development in Ulster resulted in the formation of one of the major working class areas of the British Isles, thus serving "to separate Northern Ireland permanently from mere colonial implantations, as well as from the history of Catholic, under-developed Southern Ireland."[3]

The eventual partition of Ireland was thus the outcome of the growth of two distinct Irish Peoples, each with its own view of history. Writing in 1919 James Winder Good observed that: "leaving politics aside, the special conditions of Ulster life operate in exactly the same fashion on Nationalists as on Unionists, differentiating them from their fellow-countrymen in the South, but welding Northern Protestants and Catholics into a homogenous whole . . . In speech, in temper, in outlook, the Ulsterman of all creeds contrasts more sharply with the natives of the other provinces than the Black Country does with the Home Counties; and Nationalists who refuse to admit that such a difference exists for them, are simply playing into the hands of their opponents."[4] Furthermore even by 1939 the institutions of separation themselves had had their own momentum, and while Protestants and Catholics in Ulster had not abandoned their mutual suspicions and animosities, the two communities were, in spite of themselves, being held together within an entity which was distinctive in many ways from either Great Britain or the Irish Free State.

The prevalent myth that the present situation in Ulster is due to an anti-imperialist struggle for "national liberation" has however been successfully promoted by traditional Republicans in several quarters, most particularly among socialists. Bosers Anderup comments: "The strategy of 'national liberation' which the left is presently pursuing is based on a faulty analysis and leads absolutely nowhere . . . The affirmation that Northern Irish Protestants constitute a separate national entity with a right to refuse incorporation in the Republic is usually considered to be divisive of the working class and therefore anti-socialist. On the contrary I think it is the stubborn affirmation of unity and solidarity where none exists and the extravagant claim of Irish Catholics to the whole island which is divisive. The Catholic left . . . tries to sweeten the pill for Protestants by affirming that this will be a socialist, and *ipso facto* a secular Republic. Protestants would be fools if they believed it. Socialism in Ireland is not for tomorrow. The Catholic left has demonstrated that even those who claim to constitute the socialist vanguard are trapped in nationalist ideologies."[5]

Overall there has been a widespread diffusion of the Irish Nationalist mythos, which has progressed from being a political ideal to becoming an intellectual and finally a spiritual one. Genuine loyalist and unionist fears for their ancient British heritage, for their economic well-being, for their religious freedom and last but not least for their fundamental right to self-determination have been dismissed by Nationalist apologists as "intransigence". Furthermore the basic failure of the "Northern Ireland" intelligentsia to promote the Ulster identity has led to an inevitable clash between British and Irish nationalisms. Thus the Ulster Protestants have been left to relive their past, instead of using it to build up a normal national consciousness for the present. Over and over again Derry has been beseiged and the Battle of the Boyne fought in Belfast, with the Ulster Catholics still fighting for "Ireland". Yet the complete expression of the native Ulster tradition, broader than Irish Protestantism and Catholicism, and populist in sentiment, could prepare for the political development of a new Ulster based on co-operative democracy.[6] This would allow the consensus in goverment necessary to end at last the "War in Ireland".

References

1. Henry, P. L., *Ulster Dialects*, Ulster Folk Museum (1964).

2. Evans, E. Estyn, *The Irish World*, ed. De Breffny, Thames and Hudson (1977).
3. Nairn, Tom, *The Break-up of Britain—Crisis and Neo-Nationalism*, New Left Books (1977).
4. Good, James Winder, *Ulster and Ireland*, Maunsel (London and Dublin, 1919).
5. Anderup, Bosers, "Contradictions and Struggles in Northern Ireland", in *Socialist Register,* ed. R. Miliband and G. Saville (London, 1972) p. 158, pp. 188–9.
6. Co-operative democracy means mutual aid democracy as opposed to bourgeois (liberal) democracy and the systems of state bureaucracy. It stands as the essential core of libertarianism.

"Man is appealed to, to be guided in his acts, not merely by love, which is always personal, or at the best tribal, but by the perception of his oneness with each human being. In the practice of mutual aid, which we can trace to the earliest beginnings of evolution, we thus find the positive and undoubted origin of our ethical conceptions; and we can affirm that in the ethical progress of man, mutual support—not mutual struggle—has had the leading part. In its wide extension, even at the present time, we also see the best guarantee of a still loftier evolution of our race."

Peter Kropotkin, *Mutual Aid,* 1902

"The fault is not with democracy, but that we have failed to have enough of it. If people had the opportunity to initiate community actions, they would be political; they would know that finally the way to accomplish something great is to get together with the like-minded and directly do it."

Paul Goodman, *Growing Up Absurd,* 1961

Cruithne, the legendary ancestress of the Cruthin.

CAERENI
CORNOVII
SMERTAE
LUGI
CARNONACAE DECANTAE
CREONES
CALEDONES VACOMAGI
TAEZALI
VENICONES
EPIDII DAMNONII VOTADINI
SELGOVAE
Venniconium Prom
Boreum Prom
VENNICNII ROBOGDIUM NOVANTES
DARINI
ERDINI VOLUNTII
(ULUTI) Isamnium Prom
MANAPIA BRIGANTES PARISI
NAGNATAE
EBLANI
CAUCI
DECEANGLI CORNOVII CORITANI
ICENI
MANAPII
AUTINI CORIONDI ORDOVICES TRINOVANTES
GANGANI
USDIAE BRIGANTES CATUVE LLAUNI
Sacrum Prom
VELLABORI IVERNI
Notum Prom
DEMETAE DOBUNNI
SILURES ATREBATES CANTIACI
IVERNIA BELGAE
REGNENSES
DUROTRIGES

Source: Ordnance Survey map of
Roman Britain Third Edition 1956

DUMNONII ALBION

O Miles 100

THE BRITISH ISLES ACCORDING TO PTOLEMY
Sources dated approximately 100 A.D.

CHAPTER 1

The Land of the Cruthin

The name "Ulster" ultimately derives from the ancient tribe of the "Uluti" who inhabited the North-Eastern part of Ireland in the early centuries of the Christian era. The Uluti are recorded by the geographer Ptolemy in the earliest known map of the British Isles made in the 2nd century A.D. This showed that similar British people such as the "Brigantes" lived in both Britain *and* Ireland in early times. The two islands were known to the ancient Greeks as the "Isles of the Pretani". From "Pretani" are derived both the words "Cruthin" and "Briton" for the inhabitants of these islands. The ancient British Cruthin or "Cruithne" formed the bulk of the population of both Ulster and North Britain in early Christian times and they are therefore the earliest recorded ancestors not only of the people of Ulster but of those of Scotland as well. The Cruthin later became known as Picts in North Britain.

The most ancient languages spoken in the British Isles were non-Indo-European and the progenitors of the Cruthin probably spoke one of them. The earliest mythologies of Ireland are thought to have originated from the people of the New Stone and early Bronze Ages and deal extensively with the island's divisions. The greatest achievement of these early pre-Celtic peoples, who form at least one half of our genetic make-up, were the Megalithic monuments of Newgrange, Knowth and Dowth in the Boyne Valley. The architectural and engineering skill displayed by this community, no less than the artistic sensibility demonstrated by the carved stones, bears testimony to the high degree of culture attained by them.[1] Place-name studies have also defined a later language known as Old European spoken throughout the British Isles as well as Europe. The oldest Celtic language, however, spoken in Ireland as well as Britain, was Brittonic (Old British) and this has survived as Brêton, Cornish and Welsh. Gaelic did not arrive in Ireland until *even later*, at a time when the ancient British and Gaels thought of themselves as distinct peoples.

At the height of its power the Northern Kingdom of Ulster probably stretched as far South as the Boyne River, and included the ancient Boyne Valley monuments. By the beginning of the Christian Era, when the five territories of Ireland were first taking permanent shape, Ulster had its capital at Emain Macha (Emania) now called Navan Fort, near Armagh. Invasions from the Midland Kingdom of Meath led to the disintegration of pre-historic Ulster in the 4th and 5th

1

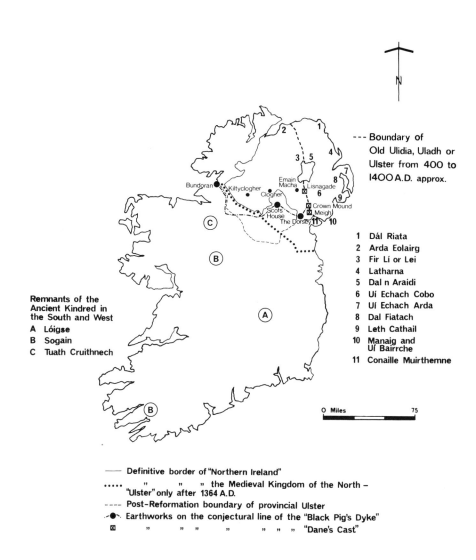

Boundary of
Old Ulidia, Uladh or
Ulster from 400 to
1400 A.D. approx.

1   Dál Riata
2   Arda Eolairg
3   Fir Lí or Lei
4   Latharna
5   Dal n Araidi
6   Uí Echach Cobo
7   Uí Echach Arda
8   Dal Fiatach
9   Leth Cathail
10 Manaig and
    Uí Bairrche
11 Conaille Muirthemne

Remnants of the
Ancient Kindred in
the South and West
A   Lóigse
B   Sogain
C   Tuath Cruithnech

O Miles   75

——— Definitive border of "Northern Ireland"
·····   "   "   " the Medieval Kingdom of the North –
    "Ulster" only after 1364 A.D.
- - - - Post-Reformation boundary of provincial Ulster
-●- Earthworks on the conjectural line of the "Black Pig's Dyke"
☒   "   "   "   "   "   "   " "Dane's Cast"

ULSTER - LAND OF THE CRUTHIN

centuries. In Mid and South Ulster there appeared the new Kingdom of Oriel (Airgialla), while in Western Ulster Owen and Connall (sons of Niall of the Nine Hostages, King of Meath) carved out a province for themselves with its capital at Aileach near Derry. The power of their descendants, the O'Neills and O'Don-nells, remained paramount in the North of Ireland from the 5th to the 12th centuries.

The ancient name of Ulster (Ulidia) survived, but during this period it was applied only to that area now known as Antrim, Down and Louth. Donegal was thoroughly colonized by the Midland Gaels and the ancient British Cruthin driven east, where they maintained their independence. This was due no doubt to the proximity of the major Pictish Kingdom in what is now known as Scotland, but which was then known as Alba. At this time the British Isles were heavily wooded and the North Channel of the Irish Sea acted not as a barrier but as a means of communication between the kindred people of Scotland and the North-Eastern part of Ireland. This inter-communication was to remain an important factor in the development of Ulster even following the conquest of the whole of the island of Ireland by the Gaels, and the imposition of the Gaelic language on its inhabitants. The Gaelic language of conquest was originally that of a ruling élite but both islands continued to be known as British Islands, Ireland having been anciently called Little Britain and Alba Great Britain. The name Gael itself is derived from the Old British "Guidel", modern Welsh "Gwyddel", meaning "Raider".

The invasion of the Midland Gaels into Ulster, and the destruction of the power of the Ulidians was to change the course of British History. The population movements which ensued resulted in settlements of Ulster "Scots" along the Western seaboard of Britain, mainly Argyll and its islands. The Venerable Bede, writing in the 8th century (*A History of the English Church and People*), states that this land was obtained from the Picts by a combination of force and treaty. These Scots gave their name to Scotland and when their Royal dynasty, in the person of Fergus MacErc, forsook the Irish Capital of Dunseverick about 500 A.D. and took up residence in Scottish Dalriada, we may assume that by this time the colony had ousted the mother-country in importance. The second point is that the 5th and 6th centuries are known to have been a period of unusually rapid development in the Gaelic language, as shown by the contrast between the general language of Ogam (Ogham) inscriptions and the earliest Old Gaelic known from manuscripts. There is little doubt that this was due to the widespread adoption of the Gaelic speech by the original inhabitants and the passage of older words and grammatical forms into Gaelic.

By this time therefore, Gaelic had, according to Heinrich Wagner, "become one of the most bizarre branches of Indo-European" since "In its syntax and general structure it has as many features in common with non-Indo-European languages, especially with Hamito-Semitic languages, as with other Indo-

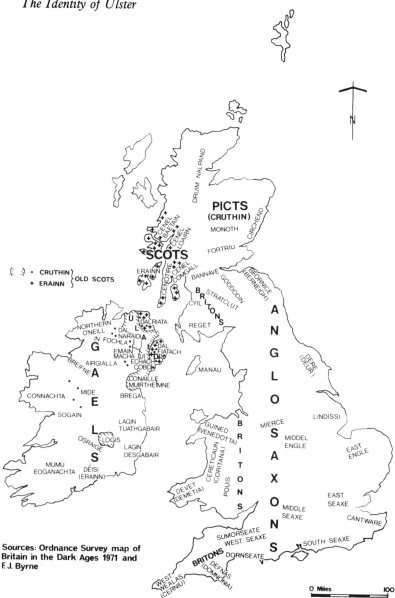

Sources: Ordnance Survey map of
Britain in the Dark Ages 1971 and
F. J. Byrne

THE BRITISH ISLES IN EARLY CHRISTIAN TIMES

European languages."[2] The language of those Irish who settled in Western Scotland was thus Gaelic and the ancient traditions of Ulster they brought with them remained strong among the common people long after they had disappeared from the greater part of Ireland. Much Ulster Folk material could still be collected in the Highlands and Islands of Scotland well into the 20th century.

In 398 A.D. St. Ninian had planted the first Christian Church in what is now Scotland at Candida Casa (now Whithorn) in Galloway. Although little is known about this great Christian Saint, or the earliest history of his foundation, it is clear that in the 5th and 6th centuries Candida Casa was an important centre of evangelism to both Britain and the Northern part of Ireland. Of the Patrick who wrote the *Confession* and *Letter to Coroticus* we have evidence of a great and holy man who loved the Scriptures well. The holy Patrick was brought in slavery to Ireland from Romanised Britain and sold to a Cruthinic chieftain called Milchu (Miliucc), who used him to tend his flocks around Mount Slemish in Co. Antrim. Thus Patrick came not among the Gaels proper (Feni) but among the Cruthin. It is said that after six years of slavery he escaped, but returned about 432 to preach the Gospel. Tradition says he stopped first at Wicklow, but not getting a good reception came north and landed in Co. Down in the territory of Dichu (of the Ulaid) who became his first convert. Dichu's barn (sabhall or Saul) near Downpatrick was the first of his churches. Patrick makes a clear distinction between the Scotti (Gaels) and the original peoples, the Hibernians (Cruthin and Ulaid). We can easily discern the old name of Ierne in the latter name. When Armagh (Ard Macha) was founded in 444 as the chief church in Ireland, Emain Macha (now Navan Fort) may still have been the political centre of the North.

Among Patrick's first converts were Bronach, daughter of Milchu and her son Mochaoi (Mahee). St. Mochaoi was to found the great monastery of Nendrum on Mahee Island in Loch Cuan (Strangford Lough), and is associated with Patrick in the legends which grew around Patrick's name. These legends firmly place Down as the cradle of Christianity in Ireland. At Nendrum were first educated Colman, who was of the Cruthin, and Finnian, who was of the Dal Fiatach (Ulaid). Colman founded in the early 6th century the famous See of Dromore in Iveagh, while Finnian, following a vist to Candida Casa, founded the great school of Movilla (Newtownards) in Down. Finnian is also notable for bringing the first copy of the Scriptures to Ireland. It is scarcely surprising that the territory nearest to Galloway should be the first to feel the evangelising influences of Candida Casa.

Founded in 555 on Ulidian territory by Comgall, perhaps the most famous of all the Cruthin, the monastery of Bangor in North Down was to become the centre of literature, both sacred and secular, in the 6th and 7th centuries. Here were to be compiled in all probability the original Chronicles of Ireland, and the beautiful poetry *The Voyage of Bran*. In this region also the old traditions of Ulster were preserved and these were moulded into the Gaelic masterpiece *The Cattle Raid of Cooley* (Táin Bó Cuailgne). The ancient Ulster Chronicle has been attributed to

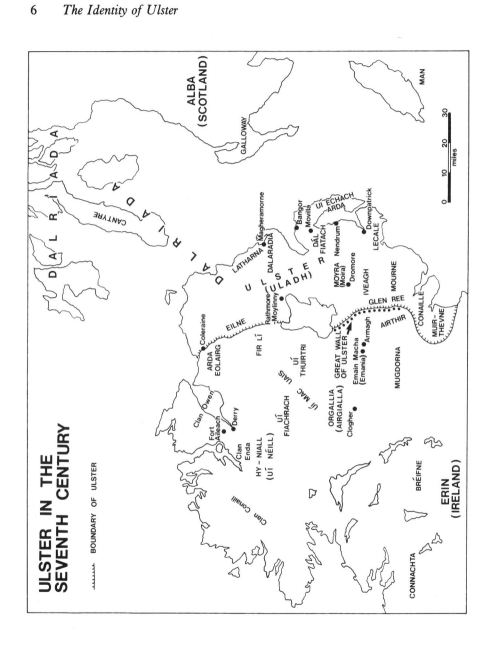

ULSTER IN THE
SEVENTH CENTURY

.... BOUNDARY OF ULSTER

ALBA
(SCOTLAND)

MAN

GALLOWAY

CANTYRE

D A L   R I A D A

UÍ ECHACH
ARDA

Bangor
Movilla

Downpatrick

LATHARNA

DÁL
FIATACH

Magheramorne

R FIATACH

Nendrum

LECALE

DALARADIA

U L S T E R
(ULADH)

MOYRA
(Moira)

Dromore

IVEAGH

MOURNE

Rathmore
-Moylinny

GLEN REE

CONAILLE

Coleraine

EILNE

FIR LÍ

GREAT WALL
OF ULSTER

AIRTHIR

MUIR–
THEVNE

ARDA
EOLAIRG

UÍ
THUIRTRI

Armagh

Emain Macha
(Emania)

MUGDORNA

Clan Owen

Derry

UÍ MAC UAIS

ORGALLIA
(AIRGIALLA)

Clogher

Fort
Aileach

UÍ
FIACHRACH

Clan
Enda

HY – NIALL
(UÍ NÉILL)

BRÉIFNE

Clan Conaill

ERIN
(IRELAND)

CONNACHTA

0   10   20   30
miles

Sinlan Moccu Min, who as Sinlanus is described in the list of abbots in the Bangor Antiphonary as the "famed teacher of the world"(famosus mundi magister). This document may be seen in the Ambrosian Library of Milan. In it we see that Patrick, Teacher of the Irish (magister Scottorum), is credited with the kindling of "a great light illuminating the World, raised on a candlestick, shining over the whole earth, a royal city well fortified and set on a hill, in which there is a great population who belong to God."[3]

Both Movilla and Bangor were great centres of scholarship, and in the 6th century many of the great scholars and saints of Ireland were educated in one or other of them. Columba (Columb-Cille), who was of the House of the Ui Neill, studied under St. Finnian at Movilla and Comgall of Bangor helped him in his work among the Picts of Alba (Modern Scotland). Columba founded in 563 the religious centres of Iona, which was to become the cultural apotheosis of Scotland. Here some scholars think the magnificent Book of Kells was executed. The followers of Columba were composed of all the peoples of Ireland, united in religion, yet we can see by Adamnan's *Life of Columba* that the Cruthin were still considered non-Gaelic at this time. From the Bangor monastery were also to come Columbanus, who founded Luxeuil in France and Bobbio in Italy, and St. Gall who founded a monastery and canton of that name in Switzerland. These were to be the chief centres of scholarship and religion which brought Europe at last out of the "Dark Ages". The glory of the Bangor Monks was the celebration of a perfected and refined *Laus Perennis* (Perennial Praise) and in singing this they entered into a covenant of mutual love and service in the Church of Jesus Christ.

In 637 Congal, Prince of the Cruthin and King of Ulster, attempted to regain the sovereignty of the whole North with the help of British allies, but was defeated and killed at the Battle of Moira in Co. Down. According to Samuel Ferguson the Battle of Moira was "the greatest battle ever fought within the bounds of Ireland. For beyond question, if Congal Claen and his Gentile allies had been victorious in that battle, the re-establishment of old Bardic paganism would have ensued".[4] As it was, pre-Christian beliefs and customs survived in the Scottish and Irish countrysides until modern times, notwithstanding the puritan piety of both Protestant Fundamentalists and Roman Catholic Ultramontanists. Eystn Evans believed that: "One should probably look to the primary Neolithic/megalithic culture rather than to the intervening Bronze Age as the main source of the Elder Faiths".[5] Evidences of pre-Celtic and Celtic custom abound throughout the Scottish–Irish cultural province, e.g. the Beltane Festival of Peebles in the Scottish Lowlands, the Oul' Lammas Fair at Ballycastle in North Antrim and Halloween everywhere. The ancient awareness of the "Good People" or "Little People" is responsible in the main for the essential unity of the peoples of North and West Britain and Ireland (wrongfully known as the "Celts") making them seem foreign to the peoples of South and East Britain (the "Anglo-Saxons"). The Battle of Moira was also important because of the resultant political cleavage between the Ulster and Scottish territories of Dalriada separating Scotia major (Ireland) from Scotia minor (the Scottish territories which were to enlarge into "Scotland"). For the next 500 years Ulster remained subservient to the medieval Kingdom of the North, although she still had her own King.

The story of the Scandanavian (Lochlan) settlements which occurred during the 9th century in Ireland and Britain is too often told from a one-sided viewpoint, in great part due to the 12th century Gaelic propaganda work *War of the Gaels with the Foreigners* (Cogadh Gaedhel re Gallaibh). Early raiding gave way to settlements and such trade and commerce that was notable in the Danish settlements of Dublin, Wexford (Veigsfjordur), Waterford, Wicklow (Vikingalo), Cork and Limerick (Hlymrekur), and in such fine literature as exemplified by the Sagas of the Norse Kings. Interaction between "stranger" "Gall" and "native" "Gael" produced in many areas (e.g. Galloway) a mixed people known as "Vikingr Scotr" to the former and "Gall-ghaedal" to the latter. As for the burning and pillaging of churches attributed by Gaelic propaganda to the Vikings, A. T. Lucas has claimed that at least half of these, from the 7th century to the 16th, were perpetrated by the Irish themselves, not only before the Vikings came, but long after the Scandanavians were absorbed into Gaelic society.[6]

Twelfth-century Gaelic propaganda was not only antagonistic to those who settled in Ireland after them, however, but to such peoples as the Cruthin who had been there before them. T. F. O'Rahilly has written in his *Early Irish History and Mythology* that: "The combined influence of Bede, Mael Mura, and the genealogical fiction of Ir, caused Cruithne to lose favour as the name of a section of the Irish population. The 12th century genealogies make no allusion to the existence of Cruthin in Ireland beyond remarking incidentally in one place that the 'Dal n Araidi are also called Cruithne'. Nevertheless the fact that there were Cruthin in Ireland as well as in Scotland was, as might be expected, long remembered; and so it is not surprising to find writers occasionally suggesting in defiance of Mael Mura, that the Cruthin of both countries formed one people in remote times."[7]

The 12th century nevertheless brought a change to a new order in Ireland, the Gaelic caste system being challenged by feudalism linked with Church reorganisation. Against this background must be judged the formal conferring of the sovereignty of Ireland on Henry II of England by the bill issued in 1155 by Pope Adrian IV, known to England as Nicolas Breakespeare, the only Englishman to have sat in "St. Peter's chair". During the subsequent Anglo-Norman, or more properly Cambro-Norman,[8] invasion of Ireland one of the baronial adventurers John de Courcy captured the Ulster capital of Downpatrick in 1177 and ruled the kingdom until dispossessed in 1205 by King John, who created Hugh de Lacy Earl of Ulster. From 1263 to 1333, the Earldom was held by the Connaught Anglo-Norman family of de Burgh or Burke, passing then to an heiress who married Lionel Duke of Clarence, a son of King Edward, and ultimately to the Crown. It was the Anglo-Normans who anglicised the name of Uladh or Ulidia to Ulster.

THE BRITISH ISLES APPROXIMATELY 1200 A.D. INDICATING THE "SCANDINAVIAN" SETTLEMENTS

Meanwhile the O'Neills and O'Donnells became virtually supreme in the North of Ireland, the former controlling mid-Ulster and much of Antrim and Down. Even under de Courcy and the Earls of Ulster, MacDonleavy (Livingston) had remained King of Ulster. With the destruction of the Anglo-Normans in the North, the O'Neills began to claim the whole of Ulster. It was not until 1364, however, that Hugh O'Neill of Tyrone was styled "King of Ulster" by the *Annals of Ulster*. Then and only then was the name Ulidia, Uladh, or Ulster applied again to the whole North and it was only in 1384 that Niall O'Neill could legitimize his claim to Ulster in the eyes of the learned classes when he held a feast for them near Emain Macha. Ulster then became the most Gaelic part of the whole island, and a bastion of the Gaelic tradition.

The two ruling clans, the O'Neills and O'Donnells, were involved in a serious rebellion against Queen Elizabeth I from 1594 to 1601 and it was only at this time that the provincial configuration of Ireland was effected with four "provinces" divided up into counties. The eastern part of the Kingdom of Breffny (Cavan) was taken from Connaught and placed artificially in Ulster while the Northern part of Louth, which had been one of the most ancient parts of Ulster, known originally at Muirtheimne and defended against the South by the legendary Ulster Warrior Setanta (Cuchulainn), was taken from Ulster and placed artificially into Leinster. The older boundaries were, however, remembered well into the 17th century. With the failure of negotiations between James I and the O'Neills and O'Donnells, several of the Gaelic chiefs including the Earls of Tyrone and Tirconnell left Ireland in 1607. This voluntary "Flight of the Earls" gave the Government the opportunity to declare their lands forfeit to the Crown.

In his *Life of Hugh O'Neill* (1845) the Young Irelander John Mitchel pointed out that: "Furthermore there was, in the 16th century, no Irish nation. Save the tie of a common language, the chieftain of Clan Connall (O'Donnell) had no more connection with the Lord of Clan Carrha (Cork), than either had with the English Pale. The Anglo-Norman colony was regarded as one of the independent tribes of the island." When Hugh O'Neill defeated the English at the Yellow Ford he was not fighting for "Ireland" in a modern nationalistic sense but in his own interest for the old Gaelic way of life. The very idea of a republican form of government would have been repugnant to the old Irish system of law. In England there had been evidences of nationalism in the reign of Henry III (died 1272) but a truly national feeling did not become a significant feature of English life until Henry V (died 1422). Elizabeth I's reign brought the flowering of English patriotism in the defeat of the Spanish Armada. Scotland in the 16th century was still a feudal monarchy and the "Gaels" of Scotland and Ireland one people.

During the 15th and 16th centuries the peoples of Carrick (Ayshire) and Galloway, although culturally Gaelic, had become classified with the Old British people of Strathclyde and the Old Angles of Lothian under the label of "Lowland Scots". The emergence of a strictly "Highland" society in Scotland as opposed to a "Lowland" one can only be dated as late as the 14th century. The social differences were originally only of emphasis: in the "Highlands" kinship was modified by feudalism and in the "Lowlands" feudalism was modified by kinship. Cultural differences were more profound, based firstly on the gradual decline of Gaelic even in Galloway and its survival in the North and West, and secondly on the formation of royal burghs in the Lowlands and the establishment of a "Middle Class" of merchants and tradesmen. Yet, contrary to popular belief, the Clan "system" remained strong in the Borders well into the 17th century. The succession of the feudal King James VI of Scotland to Elizabeth's English throne in 1603 allowed an increase in the economic well-being of Scotland and the development of a new British nationalism, out of which was born the British Empire. English nationalism, however, remained an enduring force and the history of England the premier study among the British academic élite, even in Ulster. The English themselves were most responsible for the development of Irish nationalism, since a positive romantic stereotype became necessary to counterbalance the negative stereotype they had created of everything Irish.

The ravages of the cruel and bloody War fought by the Elizabethan English against O'Neill left large areas of Ulster virtually without inhabitants. According to a contemporary account by William Camden Antrim and Down, however, already consisted for the most part of woodlands, marsh and bogland. Not long afterwards, under the influence of the new King James, many thousands of settlers, mainly Lowland Scots Presbyterians, were introduced into the new "British" "Province" of Ulster by both private settlement and public plantation.[9] The new Scottish settlers were of a different character to the earlier ones, since the Reformation in Scotland had brought a social as well as a religious transformation. The development of a strong peasant movement against the feudal lords was expressed politically in democratic ideals and culturally in the form of Presbyterianism. Those Lowland people who came to Ulster with the original title-holders (Undertakers) of land confiscated from the local Gaelic chieftains left feudalism behind them in Scotland. Using modern English methods of farming they rapidly transformed the Ulster countryside, draining in particular the drumlin country which had stood as a barrier to communication between Ulster and the rest of Ireland since prehistoric times. In extending the Scottish Lowland way of life into Ulster they were soon to see themselves as founders of a new society based on the fundamental rights of liberty, equality and fraternity.

On the other hand Padraig O Snodaigh has emphasised that "the pattern of developing events in Ulster did not depend on this Ulster Plantation alone as the 1659 survey and census show. In every county the Irish outnumbered the others though in Tyrone and Antrim the differences were not so great. The survey further shows that English (and Scots was then, incorrectly, listed as English for the purpose of the survey) was the majority language in the following areas only:— Some towns, for example Derry, Carrickfergus and Coleraine; East

Donegal; the Barony of Coleraine and the areas between Lisburn and Larne."[10] Gaelic was then "the majority" language everywhere else in Ulster. Alan Gailey has also argued: "It is possible that the 17th Century planters were forced to some degree to accommodate themselves to an existing cultural geographical pattern and that their advent to Ireland from culturally related areas (i.e. Galloway, Carrick and Inverness) meant that the plantation of Ulster as a whole was not so revolutionary as some historians have asserted, remembering that there were many settlers coming to Ulster also from culturally unrelated districts in England."[11]

Furthermore the 17th century plantation brought many Presbyterian Scots who may be justly considered as returning to the home of their ancestors. Thus F. J. Bigger has written that "When the Galloway planters came to Ulster they were only returning to their own lands like emigrants returning home again."[12] These common origins were well known to the settlers themselves as the speech made by Sir James Hamilton in the Irish House of Commons on the 1st May 1615 clearly demonstrates. Neither must it be assumed that all the settlers were Protestants, since there were Scottish Catholics as well, some of whom, such as the Hume family of the Derry area, were ultimately of English origin. Thus a letter written by the Bishop of Derry to the Lord Chancellor in the year 1629 says, "Sir George Hamilton since he got part of the Earl of Abercorn's grant of the Barony of Strabane has done his best to plant Popery there, and has brought over priests and Jesuits from Scotland." It further laments that "all the Hamilton lands are now in the hands of Papists." M. Perceval-Maxwell has confirmed that, since both Abercorn's and Sir Claud Hamilton's children were converted to Roman Catholicism through Sir George's influence, within a generation one of the most successful parts of the Scottish Plantation was led by Roman Catholics. Most other immigrants were probably at least nominally Protestant although initially their religious convictions were not strong and the development of their ideals took place in Ulster herself, depending more on local religious leaders than on previous sentiment.[13]

The new Scots settlers differed from the English in language on two counts. Firstly there was a significant group who spoke Gaelic and it seems that Scottish Gaelic speakers were intelligible to the Irish at this period. Secondly the language of the others was not the standard English of today but Lallans, which is derived from the Central Scots language, known in Scotland as "Inglis". This Lallans language is still spoken in the North – East of Ulster and in Donegal, where contact with Scotland through settlement and commerce has been close. The Scottish speech is in some ways an older form of the English language grouping than standard English and R. De Bruce Trotter in his "Galloway Gossip" has listed the chief points of difference between the two grammars.[14] Church and state have been just as antagonistic to Lallans as they have been to Gaelic itself, leading to as great a contraction of the Scots-speaking districts as the Gaelic-speaking districts of Ulster.

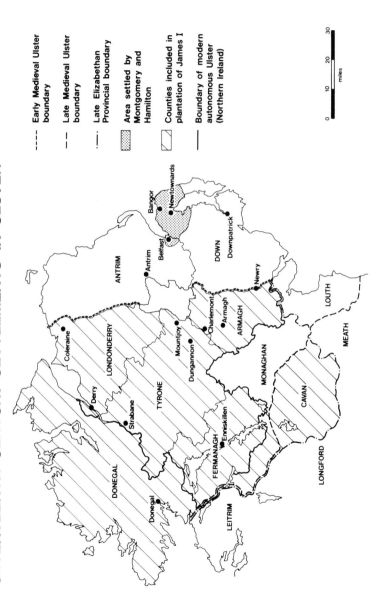

SEVENTEENTH CENTURY SETTLEMENTS IN ULSTER

THIOGHLAICTHE.

Don trinoid thoghaidhe thré pear-
fandaigh .ɪ. donathair mhor mhirbh-
aileach, & don mhac mhaiseach mhor
chumachtach, agas don fpirad naomh
nós oirrdheirc, is cóir gach vile onoir
& ghloir agas bhuidheachas do thab-
hairt tré bhioth fiór.   •

❧(✶★✶)☙

✿ DO CHVM

GACH VILE CHRISDV-
idhe ar feadh an domhain go himlan &
go hairidhe dfearaibh Alban & Eire-
and, don mheid dibh ler bhail briathra-
dífle Dé do ghabhail chuca na gcroid-
headhaibh & na nindtindibh, ata Eóin
Carfuel acur abheandachta agas
aguidhe an fpirad naomh dho
ibh odhia athar trid.
IOSA CRISD
ARDTIGH-
EARNA.

(★✝★)

DEDICATORY.

To the most excellent Trinity of three persons, viz., to the great,
marvellous Father, and to the fair, great, and powerful Son, and
to the Holy most adorable Spirit, it becomes all honour and glory
and thanks to be given, for ever and ever.

Unto every Christian throughout the whole earth, and specially to
the men of Alban (Scotland) and of Eireand (Ireland), to such of
them as desire to receive the faithful words of God in their hearts
and minds, John Carswell sends his blessing, and prays for the
Holy Spirit for them from God the Father, through
JESUS CHRIST
OUR LORD.

Extract from *The Book of Common Order, commonly called John Knox's Liturgy* translated into Gaelic by
John Carswell for the use of Presbyterians from the 16th Century onwards.

Yet Ulster as a whole was not anglicised as quickly as Leinster. According to the 1851 census, of the nine counties in Ireland which contained the least number of Gaelic speakers only one (Co. Down) was in Ulster – the other eight were in Leinster. Not only were there, at that time, twice as many Gaelic speakers in Ulster than in Leinster but each of the counties Antrim, Armagh, Londonderry, Fermanagh, and Tyrone contained more than either Carlow, Kildare, Wexford or Longford. Breandan O Buachalla has stated that in the 17th and 18th centuries there was extensive intermingling and intermarriage between the new Scottish settlers and the "native Irish" so that by the 19th century "there existed in Ulster several population groups, apart from many individuals scattered here and there, partly of Irish and partly of Scottish origin who were Irish in language and who belonged to one or other of the Protestant Churches" Estyn Evans agrees that "There was much more intermarriage, with or without the benefit of the clergy, than the conventional histories make allowance for. Many planters became Catholics and many natives became Protestants. It is an emotional oversimplification to see the plantation in terms of ruthless Protestants seizing the best stretches of land and chasing the Catholics into the bogs and hills."[15] A. T. Q. Stewart indeed believes that "a very substantial proportion of the original population was not disturbed at all."[16] Furthermore hill and bog-land, providing as they did both rough grazing and fuel, were actually the preferred environment for the old traditional rural way of life.

The fact that many "native Irish" became Protestants is well illustrated by the Hearth Money Rolls for the Presbyterian parishes of Stranorlar and Leck in Donegal for the year 1665, as well as by the presence of such old Cruthinic families as Rooney, Lowry, Macartan and Maguinness in the records of the Episcopalian Diocese of Dromore in South and West Down. Representatives of other well-known Gaelic families abound. Murphys, Maguires, Kellys, Lennons, Reillys, Doghertys and many others are quite numerous. In this Diocese of Dromore and the immediately surrounding districts the Church of Ireland bears a larger proportion numerically to the total population then perhaps in any other part of Ireland of the same area. In North Down, where 17th century settlement from Scotland was most successful, Brendan Adams has stated that "a large part of the native population became absorbed into the Protestant Church." Thus in a book listing subscribers to church funds in the Presbyterian church in Saintfield, Co. Down, at least 20% of the names were native, pre-17th century names like Dugan, Donnan, Hanvey and Kelly.[17]

Ussher's *Discourse of the Religion anciently professed by the Irish* (London 1631) also shows that many Protestants in the 17th century felt that several important points of doctrine and discipline in the early Irish Church were closer to their own religious views than those of contemporary Roman Catholicism. These sentiments continued to be expressed by prominent Protestants down to modern times, notably by the Presbyterian historian James Seaton Reid in his *History of the Presbyterian Church in Ireland* (1833) and by the Gaelic scholar Nigel Mac-Neill in his *Literature of the Highlanders* (1892). A great lover of the Bangor Antiphonary Mac Neill described the early Irish Church as "the primitive Free Church". For him there was no doubt that "The Gaels of Ireland and Scotland were the same people, having the same language and music; and all the elements of civilisation about them were the common property of both. At the same time there are evidences that the Gaels of the North of Ireland stood in closer relationship to those of Scotland than those in the South of Ireland. And this holds true even to this very day."

References

1. O'Kelly, Claire, *Newgrange, Co. Meath*, Cork (1985).
2. Wagner, Heinrich, *Studies in the origins of the Celts and of early Celtic civilisation* (Belfast – Tubingen, 1971).
3. Adamson, Ian, *Bangor, Light of the World*, Fairview Press (Bangor, 1979).
4. Ferguson, Samuel, *Congal – The Battle of Moira*, Belfast (1980).
5. Evans, E. Estyn, *The Personality of Ireland*, Blackstaff Press (1981).
6. Lucas, A. T. "The plundering and burning of Churches in Ireland", in Rynne (ed.), *North Munster Studies* (Limerick, 1967).
7. O'Rahilly, T. F., *Early Irish History and Mythology* (Dublin, 1964).
8. Hyde, D., *A Literary History of Ireland*, T. Fisher Unwin (1901). It should be remembered that the Norman conquest of England and Wales was a relatively recent one at this time. The Norman French had many Brêtons among them whose Old British heritage remained strong enough to make them believe that they were avenging their ancient defeat by the Anglo-Saxons. Those who settled among the Welsh found an identical heritage to their own. Geoffrey de Monmouth (*c.* 1100–1155) was very proud of his British heritage and his *Historia Regum Britanniae* or *History of the Kings of Britain* furnished the Welsh and Brêtons with the national history they desired. When Richard de Clare, Earl of Pembroke, landed at Waterford on 23rd August, 1170 he brought with him a Cambro-Norman army which was far from "English" in culture, language or ethnic origin. The Old British or Irish hero Arthur soon became adopted by the English just as the Ancient British hero Setanta became gaelicised into Cuchulainn, then briticised again, finally appearing in the masterpiece of medieval alliterative poetry as *Sir Gawain and the Green Knight*. See Brian Stone's Penguin Classic, 1959.
9. Before 1610, thousands of other Scots left the poverty of their homeland to seek their fortune on the Continent. William Lithgow, who visited Poland in 1616, called it "Mother and Nurse for the youth and younglings of Scotland, who are yearly sent hither in great numbers, thirty thousand Scots families that live incorporate in her bowells." While this sounds excessive it indicates a large influx. Bruno Fuchs has estimated that "some 2,500 Scottish families sought their fortunes in East Prussia, West Prussia and Pomerania between 1500 and 1700. There had been officers of the Scots Brigade in Dutch service for three hundred years." Scottish Historical Review XXVII (1948), 187.
10. O Snodaigh, Padraig, *Hidden Ulster* (Dublin, 1977).
11. Gailey, Alan, "Cultural Connections in North-West Britain and Ireland", *Ethnologia Europa*, vol. ii–iii, p. 139.
12. Bigger, F. J. "From Uladh to Galloway and From Galloway to Uladh", *The Red Hand Magazine*, vol. 1, no. 3, Nov., 1920, p. 22.
13. Perceval-Maxwell, M., *The Scottish Migration to Ulster in the Reign of James I*, Routledge and Kegan Paul (1973).

14. Trotter, De Bruce R., *Galloway Gossip* (Dumfries, 1901).
15. Evans, E. Estyn, *The Personality of Ireland*, Blackstaff Press (1981).
16. Stewart, A. T. Q., *The Narrow Ground, Patterns of Ulster History*, Pretani Press (1986).
17. Adams, Brendan, *The Hand is Red* by Biggs-Davison, Johnson (London, 1973).

THE BRITISH ISLES APPROXIMATELY 1700 A.D. ILLUSTRATING THE CIVIL WARS OF THE THREE KINGDOMS

CHAPTER 2

The Wars of the Three Kingdoms

It was to be primarily the religious differences that were to shape the allegiances of the Ulster people as a whole in the centuries following the plantation. Wars of Religion were now raging all over Europe and the Rhineland in particular was suffering the devastation of the Thirty Year's War. Roman Catholic reaction was centred around the Hapsburg Dynasty, first as rulers of Spain and then as rulers of Austria and the Holy Roman Empire. Scandinavia and the North German States were bulwarks of Protestantism and for the time being France's large Huguenot population was protected by the benign Edict of Nantes. It was thus natural that the Catholic Irish should look towards Southern Europe for support. It was just as natural for the Protestant Irish to fear such support and seek to destroy it. Sermons on morality should not enter into the discussion, since each side suffered as much as the other. The important result, as far as Ulster was concerned, was that the rise of Protestantism led to a political fusion of the Catholic recusants of Ireland, and a mutal antagonism between sections of the people of Ulster which has lasted until this day.

The accession of Charles I of England in 1625 allowed Catholics to negotiate concessions ("Graces") concerning such questions as land tenure and religion, in return for an annual payment to the King's Exchequer. No family could be dispossessed if it had held its lands for more than sixty years. The Oath of Supremacy was replaced by a simple oath of allegiance for those Catholics seeking to practise law, and was not now essential as a prerequisite for Wards of Court to come into their inheritance. In 1633 Charles I made Thomas Wentworth Lord Deputy of Ireland, and William Laud became Archbishop of Canterbury. Both men were to cause sore affliction to fall on the Presbyterians of Ulster. Under Laud's High Church influence a convocation of the Church of Ireland at length accepted the Thirty-Nine Articles of the Church of England. A loyal vassal of his Absolute Monarch, Wentworth laid down as one of his policies the religious conformity of the whole of Ireland, and strongly supported Laud's stipulations. The result was that those Ulster ministers such as John Livingstone of Antrim, who would not conform, were forced to return to Scotland. There they streng-thened the resistance to Laud's Liturgy, that "Popish-English-Scottish-Mass-

Service-Book" as it was locally described. In 1637 this resistance burst out into rebellion and resulted in the Scottish Covenant so widely accepted in Galloway. For the next five years most Scottish congregations in Ulster were without their ministers, and as many as five hundred crossed the Irish Sea on one occasion to celebrate the Lord's Supper under the exiled Livingstone at Stranraer in Galloway.

In 1638 Livingstone represented Wigtownshire at the notable Glasgow meeting of the General Assembly of the Church of Scotland which abolished the Bishops, the Articles of Perth, the Book of Canons and the Prayerbook. Such actions were in total defiance of Charles I, and by the Spring of 1639 war between the King and Covenanters was inevitable. Wentworth was determined that no such defiance would take place among the kindred Scots of Ulster, and therefore tried to impose on them the "Black Oath", by which they would swear to obey the King's royal commands, and would declare against the Scottish rebellion. Those who refused returned to Scotland. Furthermore, when Wentworth (now Lord Strafford) learned that Charles was planning to invade Scotland in 1640, he raised an army in Ireland of nine thousand to help the King. The majority of these were Catholics. All this was totally unacceptable to the increasingly powerful Parliamentarians in England and there was also a call to arms by the Army of the Covenant in Scotland. Opposition to Strafford grew as the power of Charles declined, and the English Parliament finally had him attainted and executed on 12th May, 1641.

The opportunity offered to the Catholic Irish by civil unrest in England, as well as fear engendered by the Puritan aspect of the new English Parliament, led inevitably to a rebellion in Ireland later that year. The plans for this were worked out by a member of one of the last Cruthinic families in Southern Ireland, gaelicised more than a millenium before. The O'Mores, or Moores, were among the final remnants of the Loigse, who had held the territory named from them, Laois (in English form "Leix"), a portion of the Leinster county now so named (formerly Queen's county). The Loigse had been ruled by the Moores from the earliest documentary period until they lost their lands in the English plantation of the 15th century. It was primarily against the more recent, and therefore Protestant, English settlers and the Dublin Government that Rory O'More directed the first assault in October 1641. Prominent among his fellow conspirators were northern malcontents led by Sir Phelim O'Neill and with him was Sir Con Magennis of Iveagh. Within a few weeks the Anglo-Normans and other Hiberno-English of the Pale joined the insurrection on the side of the rebels. This union of Old English Catholics with Gaelic Catholics was the real beginning of Catholic nationalism in Ireland. About one quarter of the genes of the people of Eire are derived in fact from Catholic Anglo-Norman and English settlers. The most common surname in Eire is Walsh or Welsh, which derives from West Britain.

It was the declared policy of the rebels at the beginning of the uprising that the Scottish Presbyterians should be left alone because of their "Gaelic" origins.

Thus Colonel Audeley Mervyn, in a report presented to the House of Commons in June, 1642, states that: "In the infancy of the Rebellion the rebels made open proclamations, upon pain of death, that no Scotchman should be stirred in body, goods or lands, and that they should to this purpose write over the lyntels of their doors that they were Scotchmen, and so destruction might pass over their families." Furthermore he related that he had read a letter, "sent by two of the rebels, titulary colonels, Colonel Nugent and Colonel O'Gallagher . . . which was directed to, 'Our honourable friends, the gentlemen of the never conquered Scotch nation.'" However the conflict quickly became a sectarian one, and the distinction between the Scottish and English Protestant settlers was not long maintained. The English settlers suffered most, nevertheless, and many thousands lost their lives both in the fighting itself and in the privation which followed.

By February 1642 only a few areas remained in the hands of the Protestants. The Ulster Scots held North Down and South Antrim, including the town of Belfast and the walled city of Carrickfergus. The towns of Coleraine, Londonderry and Enniskillen were also defended without difficulty, as was North Donegal. In the South, however, only Dublin, Drogheda, Cork and a few scattered outposts remained under government control. Sir Phelim O'Neill claimed that he was acting under the authority of Charles I, and exhibited as proof a commission under the Great Seal of England. Although such a claim was undoubtedly untrue, suspicion of the King's complicity was not easily refuted in England and Scotland. In March 1642 Charles gave his assent to an Act of the English Parliament which promised any "Adventurers" who would contribute funds for the War, repayment in confiscated Irish Land. Although most of the money so accumulated was actually used later by the Parliament to finance its war with the King himself, the Adventurers were to form an influential group in the suppression of the rebellion and the subsequent settlement of Ireland under Cromwell.

In April 1642 the Presbyterians were relieved by a new Scottish Army under Major General Monro, who landed at Carrickfergus. In May the Confederate Catholics met at Kilkenny, where they set up a provisional government. In June, however, Monro took the offensive and drove back the Northern Catholic forces, recapturing Newry, Mountjoy and Dungannon. Rebel hopes rose again, nevertheless, with the arrival of their natural leader, Owen Roe O'Neill, in Lough Swilly towards the end of July. Shortly afterwards Thomas Preston, an Anglo-Irish Catholic leader, arrived at Waterford and was well received in the Pale. Both men had achieved military reputations in the Spanish Netherlands, and their personal rivalries highlighted the ill-concealed distrust between the pre-Norman and Anglo-Irish factions. In August civil war broke out in England between King and Parliament, and the loyalties of the Protestant Parliament in Dublin were divided between the two parties. The Confederation of Kilkenny, on the other hand, met in October 1642 and adopted the motto *Pro Deo, Pro Rege, Pro Patria Hibernia Unanimio*, declaring in effect, their loyalty to the King.

Following the indecisive Battle of Edgehill at the end of October, the King entered Oxford in triumph, but, mindful of the army of the Catholic Confederacy, at length in January 1643 secretly ordered his Irish representatives, Ormonde and Clanricarde, to enter into negotiations with the rebels. Ormonde, who was of the Butler family, was a Protestant Anglo-Irishman of Norman origins and had many relatives among the Anglo-Norman element of the rebel army. Although these Anglo-Irish Catholics were willing to reach an agreement with Ormonde, the pre-Norman Irish were satisfied by the official Papal Agent, Father Scarampi, that they could win an outright victory. Thus dissension ensued. In September 1643 a truce was finally arranged between Ormonde and the Confederacy, but this was denounced outright by Monro, who subsequently signed the Solemn League and Covenant with his fellow Scots and the English Parliamentarians. The Scottish Covenanters had been waiting for such a truce ever since the Earl of Antrim was caught returning to Ireland from England with letters concerning a scheme to raise his clan, the Catholic MacDonnells (MacDonalds) of Ulster, for an invasion of Scotland on behalf of the King. They were proved right again by the uprising of the great Scottish Royalist, James Graham, Marquis of Montrose, who raised the Scottish Highlanders[1] and, with a fine body of their relatives from the Isles and Ulster sent by Antrim, went from victory to victory over the Covenant. In 1645, however, the English Parliamentarians under Oliver Cromwell won the decisive Battle of Naseby against Charles and when Montrose was finally defeated at Philiphaugh, near Selkirk, in September 1645 by the Covenant Army, the power of the Cavaliers fast ebbed away. The period of the "First Civil War" of the Three Kingdoms finally ended when Charles surrendered to the Scots on 5th May 1646.

By this time the new Papal Nuncio, John Rinnuccini, Archbishop of Fermio, was providing funds from the Vatican for the Catholic Army of Ulster under Owen Roe O'Neill. In June 1646, this trained force won a notable victory over Monro at Benburb in County Armagh. If O'Neill had then pressed on to Carrickfergus he would have probably won Ulster. Instead he chose to remain inactive for some months, acting only when the negotiations of the Kilkenny Supreme Council with Ormonde were not going to his liking. Finally at the end of September he marched South to Kilkenny and, joining up with Preston, dissolved the Council and installed Rinnuccini as the President of a new one. Ormonde continued to bargain with both Preston and Sir James Dillon of Athlone, but was thwarted for the moment by the sagacity of the superior O'Neill. Eventually he saw his best purpose was to come to terms with Michael Jones, the Parliamentary commander in Ireland, so he handed over Dublin to Jones, returned to England and reported to the King, who was now a prisoner of the English Parliament.

Time was running out for Charles, who at last decided to play his King of Scots card with the Covenanters, for, whatever his religious or political beliefs, he was a Stuart.[2] Under the influence of the more moderate Covenanters ("Engagers") led by the Duke of Hamilton, the Scottish army, which included several of the Monro's Ulster regiments, invaded England and were utterly defeated by the New Model Army under Cromwell at Preston early in 1648.

This reopening of the Civil War, or Second Civil War as it is sometimes called, caused a complete change of allegiance in Ulster. Ormonde considered that the time was now right for him to return again to Ireland as, with the disaffection of Inchiquin, Lord President of Munster, as well as the Scots, from the Parliamentary side and the support of the Catholic Anglo-Irish, he saw an opportunity to save two of the Three Kingdoms for the King. So, leaving the Queen in France, he set sail for Ireland and towards the end of September 1648 reached Kilkenny. There he formally dissolved the Confederacy and declared Rinnuccini a rebel, forcing him to leave the country. The Parliamentary forces were quick to respond. Monck and Coote secured Carrickfergus and Londonderry from Monro and Stewart respectively, thus keeping the Ulster Scots in check. In Scotland, too, the Covenanters of Galloway and Ayrshire marched on Edinburgh with 6,000 men to demand that there should be no more negotiating with the King. These protesters were known as Whigs, and gave their name to the great political party. Events reached their climax in 1649, when Charles was tried and executed in London.

References

1. The Highlanders were still known to the Scottish Government as "Irish" and yet in Ireland as "Scotch": see Scottish Covenanters and Irish Confederates by David Stevenson, Ulster Historical Foundation (Belfast, 1981). The Gallowegians were called "Irish" by the English army at the Battle of the Standard in 1138.
2. The Stuart (Stewart) family had in the main line occupied the ancient throne of the Scots for upwards of three hundred years. This famous but ill-fated house sprang from a Brêton (Old British) nobleman named Alan son of Flaald who was contemporary with William the Conqueror. Alan's son Walter obtained from David I the high office of Steward of Scotland. A descendant, Robert, the son of the Stewart by Margory Bruce, succeeded to the crown on the death of his nephew, David II, in 1371. The Scottish and thus British monarchy is also descended from that of the Picts and Scots. It can ultimately be traced back to Fergus Mac Erc of Dalriada and the Pictish Kings. The name of Carrickfergus town means "Rock of Fergus".

Covenanter Field Meeting.

CHAPTER 3

The Covenanters

News of the beheading of Charles was received with revulsion by Covenanters of all shades of opinion in both Scotland and Ulster. The Belfast Presbytery drew up a "Representation" in February condemning "the Sectarian Party" of the English Parliament as "proceeding without rule of example to the trial of the King and as putting him to death with cruel hands." It must be said, however, that, in stirring up a Second Civil War, Charles had probably forfeited his right to live. Following the King's death, Ormonde immediately proclaimed Charles II King at Cork and continued the war in the name of the new King in April 1649. Enniskillen then declared for the King. Monro escaped his English captors and led his beloved Scots again. Joining with Clanricarde he took Sligo. At this point O'Neill and Monck agreed to a local truce, but were defeated by Inchiquin at Dundalk. Unfortunately for the Royalists, however, the Parliamentary forces in Dublin were reinforced now by 2,000 Ironside veterans, and on 2nd August 1649 Jones defeated Ormonde's army at Rathmines, just south of that city. A fortnight later Oliver Cromwell arrived in Dublin to settle his accounts and to restore this "Bleeding Nation of Ireland to its former happiness and tranquillity". His campaign was exactly what he meant it to be – quick and cruel, but effective. The actual events have been much coloured by restoration propaganda.

Cromwell's campaign against the Royalist forces began with the storming of Drogheda on 11th September 1649. The subsequent massacre involved primarily the English Royalist garrison and there is no foundation for the later fictions of indiscriminate slaughter of the whole civilian population. The fall of Drogheda was enough, however, to persuade O'Neill that the time had come for an alliance with Ormonde but this made little difference to the Ironsides, now the finest army in Europe. In October they took Wexford and, on finding evidence of atrocities committed against the town's Protestant inhabitants, gave no quarter to the Irish garrison. By the end of November O'Neill had died and the only Ulster strongholds left in Royalist hands were Charlemont and Enniskillen, while the Protestant Royalist garrisons of Cork, Youghal and Kinsale had joined Cromwell of their own volition. When the Lord Lieutenant and General for the Parliament of England left Ireland on 26th May 1650 he was confident that his deputies would be able to finish the war soon, and that the Gaelic aristocracy was doomed, its caste system of social order destroyed for all time. He left in command the fine soldier, Henry Ireton.

25

But now Cromwell had to face the Scottish Lion in the North. The Covenanters were angered by the beheading of the King and the increasing coolness of the Puritan party towards Presbyterianism. Accordingly a deputation had been sent, first to the Hague, and then to Breda, for the purpose of laying before the dissolute young Charles II the conditions on which they would accept him as King. These he accepted but he was never to forgive the humiliation. In the Summer of 1650 he journeyed to Scotland and on 16th August signed the Declaration of Dunfermline acknowledging his own and his father's sins in opposing the Covenant, and admitting the "exceeding great sinfulness of that treaty and peace made with the bloody Irish rebels, who treacherously shed the blood of so many of his faithful and loyal subjects in Ireland." This so compromised Ormonde that it spelled the end of the precarious union of Royalists in Ireland. For Charles it meant a Covenant Army, well over 1,000 men of whom were Gallowegians. They proved no match for Cromwell, who defeated them at Dunbar on 3rd September 1650. Ormonde sailed for France on 11th December leaving Clanricarde as his deputy, for he felt his presence was now an embarrassment to his cause. The following year Charles II was defeated at Worcester and also retired into exile in France. The War in Ireland continued for almost two years more. Clanricarde finally surrendered on 28th June 1652 and was allowed to retire to his English estate at Somerhill in Kent. When Inishbofin Island surrendered early in the following year, Rory Moore, last of the Loigse Cruthin, made his way secretly to Ulster, Land of the Cruthin, where he lived out his days in seclusion as a fisherman.

Cromwell's designs for the conquered Ireland were embodied in an Act of Settlement passed by the "Long Parliament" in England in August 1652. This provided for an extensive forfeiture of land in Ulster, Leinster and Munster, 10 counties of which were set aside to repay the "Adventurers" and to remunerate the Parliamentary soldiers. While the leaders of the rebellion had forfeited all rights to their land and property, all others who had not "manifested their constant good affection to the Commonwealth of England" were to suffer partial forfeiture, losing one fifth, one third or two thirds of their estates, according to the degree of their "delinquency". A scheme was made whereby they would be obliged to accept lands in Connacht and Clare equal in value to the land which remained to them. The Irish prisoners-of-war were allowed to enlist in the service of European nations and about 40,000 did so, chiefly going to Spain. Some two hundred persons were executed for their parts in the massacre of 1641, among them Sir Phelim O'Neill. Catholic priests were transported to the West Indies. The Episcopalians also suffered, as did the Presbyterians of Antrim and Down, for it was decided that they should be transported south, away from the Scottish mainland and continued support from Ayrshire (Carrick) and Galloway. Cromwell indeed drove all the Anglican bishops out of Ireland and every Presbyterian minister with the exception of five – two of them being Ker of Ballymoney and O'Quinn of Billy.

Although it was first announced that all "transplantable" persons should remove themselves by 1st May 1654 and that they should be liable to death if they didn't, permission to delay for individuals was freely given. In April 1653, Cromwell dissolved the Rump Parliament and ruled as Lord Protector, and a change of policy towards the leading Ulster Scots meant that their transportation south was not carried into effect. Neither was the subsequent settlement of Ireland by Cromwellian soldiers a success, for not only did they need the Irish tenants but, despite strict attempts to prevent them, they intermarried with the Catholic Irish and within a generation many became Catholics and fought for the Jacobite cause. W. B. Stanford has written of the shock to "Irish racialists when haematological experts asserted that blood-tests proved Aran islanders to be descended from British soldiers",[1] presumably Cromwell's garrison of Fensmen.

The only lasting effect of the Cromwellian Settlement as a whole was the complete fusion of the pre-Normans and Anglo-Irish, but this amalgam was Gaelic in language only. In 1654 Cromwell despatched his son, Henry, to be ruler of Ireland and under his firm but mild government an increase in liberty was granted to Catholic, Presbyterian and Episcopalian alike, and Ireland began to prosper again. During the remaining years of the Protectorate the ministers of the devout Covenanting sect gained a tremendous hold over the people of Galloway and Ayrshire. This was to have a profound influence on following events. Ministers were allowed to return to Ulster. An Irish State Paper of 1660 states that "there are 40,000 Irish and 80,000 Scots in Ulster ready to bear arms, and not above 5,000 English in the whole province besides the army."

Following the death of Cromwell there was a year of anarchy, brought to a close by the restoration of Charles II in 1660. Charles's first act was to restore the Episcopalian Church in the Three Kingdoms, and in 1661 an Act of Conformity was passed which required every minister who officiated in a Parish church to confirm to the Episcopal Church and the Prayer Book. "Nonconformist" ministers were ejected from their churches (in all, sixty-four). Persecution of the Galloway Presbyterians had to wait for a year, since Charles was aware that in Scotland he would have to progress in stages. In the Autumn of 1661, however, the former Presbyterian minister of Crail, James Sharp, accepted the post of Archbishop of St. Andrews, Primate of Scotland, and the Parliament of 1662 confirmed the return of prelacy.

Throughout most of Scotland the ministers submitted, but not so in Galloway. There the people resisted and this resistance resulted between 1662 and 1666 in the economic ruin of Galloway. Government troops under Sir James Turner occupied and terrorised the whole area. Courts of High Commission were re-introduced and hundreds of covenanters were fined, imprisoned, tortured or deported to the Colonies. Eventually this could no longer be borne, and on 13th November 1666 the "Pentland Rising" was initiated at Dalry. On November 21st a Covenanter force of about 1,000 men assembled at the Brig O'Doon near Ayr and marched on Edinburgh. On 28th November at Rullian Green, at the foot of the Pentland hills, they were routed, and many fled to Ulster and Holland. Following the Rising the persecution of Galloway was increased under Sir William Bannatyne whose followers' murders, rapes and robberies were so numerous that the Government itself became sickened. In 1669 the Act of Indulgence was proffered to the Gallowegians, but it was not enough for them and only four ministers in the whole of Galloway subscribed to it.

In Ulster, on the other hand, the Presbyterians had learnt to live with the prelacy as they had done before and because of this Charles II was so well disposed towards them that he granted to the Ulster ministers a Regium Donum or Royal Bounty. So, for the twelve years following 1670, there was really nothing that could be remotely described as persecution in Ulster. It was this difference between the two regions which resulted in an influx from Galloway of many of her impoverished citizens.

On 13th August 1670 the Scottish Government passed the notorious "Black Act" which made field preaching an offence punishable by death. To this barbarous legislation the increasingly impoverished Hill Folk of Galloway uttered a defiance whose fire the Government attempted to extinguish in blood. In 1678 the arrival of the Highland Host under James Graham of Claverhouse marked the beginning of a grim final decade of persecution in Galloway. These Highlanders were "authorised to take free quarter, to seize all horses for carrying their sick men, ammunition and other provisions and are idemnified against all pursuits, civil and criminal, for anything they do whether killing, wounding, apprehending, or imprisoning such as shall make opposition to authority."

When the Highlanders returned to their homes at seedtime, as was the custom of such Gaelic raiding parties, their place was taken by English dragoons under their own officers, who gave orders to shoot on sight. On Sunday 1st June 1679 Claverhouse and his troops attacked a field meeting or conventicle at Drumclog, but was defeated by the Covenanters. On 22nd June, however, a badly-led army of Covenanters were defeated at Bothwell Bridge. Following this a merciless persecution of Galloway was initiated. A Test Act was passed in August 1681 which obliged them to accept the complete authority of the King in all matters civil and ecclesiastical and to renounce Presbyterianism. Courts were set up to enforce this, and these were presided over by Claverhouse's brothers and Sir Robert Grierson of Lagg. Innocent, suspected and guilty alike were subjected to extreme torture and then either imprisoned on the Bass Rock, or in Blackness Castle. Many others were transported to the colonies to be sold as slaves. Of these events Claverhouse wrote, "In the meantyme we quartered on the rebelles, and endevoured to destroy them by eating up their provisions, but they quickly perceived the dessein, and soued their corns on untilled ground. After which we fell in search of the rebelles, played them hotly with pairtys, so that there were severall taken, many fleid the country and all were dung from their hants; and

The Battle of Drumclog.

rifled so their houses, ruined their goods, and imprisoned their servants, that their wyfes and childring were broght to sterving; which forced them to have recourd to the safe conduct, and mid them glaid to renounce their principles." The courts continued their work until all the Scottish prisons were full and those who escaped hanging were transported into slavery in the West Indies.

In October 1684 James Renwick of Moniaive assumed the leadership of the Covenanters and published his Apologetical Declaration against the king and his ministers. The Government replied immediately by an Abjuration Oath renouncing the Declaration, which was to be taken in addition to the Test all over the South-west. At the same time the Privy Council passed an Act which stated that; "The Lords of his majesty's Privy Council do hereby ordain any person who owns, or will not disown, the late treasonable document (the Apologetical Declaration), whether they have arms or not, to be immediately put to death". This opened the way for summary execution without trial and the following period, covering the Autumn of 1684 and the whole of 1685, became known as the "Killing Times". Although by this time a milder persecution had returned to Ulster, that area had continued to prosper especially in Antrim and Down. Galloway itself continued to decline economically and for the following fifty years was easily the most depressed area in Scotland. In fact, not only was trade virtually non-existant, but the harvests were often so bad that a state of famine existed. The people became so poor that the names Gallowegian and Kreenie, which derives from Cruithne (Cruthin), became terms of deprecation, although the latter term continued to be used in Galloway down to the 19th century.

"Galloway Gossip", printed in 1901, describes the Hill Folk of Galloway as follows: "Yin o' the Hill country breeds is whut some folk consithers the descendants o' the Picts; an if that's the case, than the Picts wusna a bonnie folk, that's a'. This breed's no confine't tae Gallawa, for they hae them a' ower the North o' Airlan, amang the muntins o'Perthshire, an ower maist the haill o' Aiberdeenshire, an through naur a' the hill country o' the north. They even hae o' them in Englan". "And again Ey. There's the Kreenies or Gossocks too.[2] They'r no unlike the first kin' o' Hill folk, only they'r no sae big. Some folk says they wur yince Morroughs, an that's hoo the women haes beards; and some says they'r the descendants o' the Eerish Picts; but A'm no saying. The feck o' them inhabits the Rhinns."[3] Modern place-name studies of the Rhinns indicate Gaelic-speaking settlement from Ulster to Galloway since pre-Norse times.[4] Migration back again in the 17th century was merely part of an ongoing process. Furthermore the growing prosperity and relative religious tolerance of Ulster during this period attracted not only the remnants of the impoverished Galloway people, but also Puritans, Quakers and other Dissenters, mainly from the Northern Counties of England and especially from Yorkshire and Durham. These settlers were to leave their own impression on the language and personality of Ulster.

References
1. Stanford, W. B., *The Riddle of Elba*, Irish Times, 19th May, 1979.
2. "I suggest that the Kreenies were by origin Cruithnean (Cruthin) settlers, probably fishermen and very small farmers, from Dál Araide (Dalaradia, Ulster), just the people, in fact, who might be called Gossocks, 'servile people', by the Cumbric natives whom they found in Galloway." John MacQueen in "Welsh and Gaelic in Galloway," *Transactions of the Dumfriesshire and Galloway Natural History and Antiquarian Society*. Third series, vol. xxxii (Dumfries, 1955).
3. Trotter, De Bruce, R., *Galloway Gossip* (Dumfries, 1901).
4. Nicolaisen, W. F. H., *Scottish Place-Names*, Batsford (London, 1976).

Key: 1–2 Londonderry, 3 Cathedral Mounted with Guns, 4 Bishop's Street, 5 New Bastions, 6 Town Hall, 7 The Harbour, 8 Provision Ships including *Mountjoy* in Harbour, 9 *The Darmouth*, 10 *The Jerusalem*, 11 *The Phoenix*, 12 *The Long*, 13 Culmore, 14 Boom broken by *Mountjoy*, 15 Assault on the Windmill. A–B Kirke's Fleet, C Irish Jacobites surprised by the inhabitants of Inch, D Arrival of Irish Jacobites, E Sortie against the Irish Jacobites and their defeat, F French works incomplete, G French approaches, H French works destroyed, I French and Irish fighting, K Cruelties of King James and D'Avaux executed on the Clergy.

CHAPTER 4

The Glorious Revolution

The year 1685 was a year of destiny, not only for the people of Ulster and Galloway, but for the British peoples as a whole. On 6th February Charles II died as a Roman Catholic and his brother James II ascended the throne. At this time the inhabitants of the growing town of Belfast (pop. 2,000) sent a congratulatory address to the new King. But James was an avowed Roman Catholic, and his three year's reign and its immediate aftermath constituted the greatest threat yet to the new settlers. The fears of the whole Protestant population in Ireland were first engendered by the recall of Ormonde, whose Protestant sympathies were not in accord with James's design for Ireland. According to Lord Macauley, James also "obtained from the obsequious estates of Scotland, as the surest pledge of their loyalty, the most sanguinary law that has ever in our island been enacted against Protestant Nonconformists."[1] With this law and the dragoons of Claverhouse he wasted and oppressed Galloway still more, the atrocities culminating with the foul murder of the Wigton Martyrs, Margaret Maclachlan and Margaret Wilson in May.

In England, however, James was forced to tread warily. The Duke of Monmouth, natural son of Charles II, was alive and well, an exile in Holland, and a claimant for the throne. Along with Monmouth's supporters were the refugee Scots under the Earl of Argyle, MacCallum More, Chief of the Clan Campbell. MacCallum More returned to Scotland in June and tried to raise his clan for the Presbyterian cause, but was captured and executed. A merciless vengeance was then wrought by his conquerors on the people of Argyle. Athol hanged as many Campbells as he could, and the country around Inverary was laid waste to an extent of thirty miles. Meanwhile Monmouth had landed in the West country of England where, after a short campaign, he was defeated at the Battle of Sedgemoor on July 15th. Following this the Bloody Assizes opened by Judge Jeffreys against Monmouth's followers made James's name hated throughout the West Country.

Although thus triumphant, James's Catholic Design was ironically thwarted by anti-Protestant legislation enforced by his cousin, Louis XIV of France. The Revocation of the Edict of Nantes suppressed all the privileges granted by Henry IV and Louis XII to the Huguenots, inhibited the exercise of the Protestant religion, enjoined the banishment of all its ministers within 15 days, held out rewards for converts, and prohibited keeping schools, or bringing up children, in any but the Catholic religion. Dragoons were sent into Languedoc, Dauphine and Provence to enforce the decree, and it has been estimated that some half-million Huguenots left France as a result. They migrated mostly to the British Isles, Holland and Germany, and brought with them their arts, industry and resentment. Their most persistent memory was the wholesale massacre of Huguenots on St. Bartholomew's Day, 24th August, 1572 by order of the Queen-Mother, Catherine de' Medici.

Most important, perhaps, of those who left France for Holland was the Duke of Schomberg, who was a Marshal of France. At this time the Stadholder of the Dutch Republic was William, Prince of Orange, who was married to James II's elder daughter, Mary. William's acceptance of Schomberg as the general of his armies was to have important consequences for Ulster. Ulster was also to receive many Huguenots, whose Calvinist form of worship made their assimilation into the Presbyterian community a rapid one. It is interesting to note that those who came from the Protestant Orange district in Southern France owed an allegiance to William's house which can be dated as far back as the 8th century. However, as far as the Catholic Design was concerned the flood of persecuted Protestants into England made James's task well-nigh impossible.

In Ireland, nevertheless, James felt he could progress as planned. In 1686 he appointed his brother-in-law, Clarendon, Lord Lieutenant of Ireland, and Richard Talbot, an ardent Roman Catholic, both Earl of Tyrconnell and General of the Forces in the island. Tyrconnell proceeded to dismiss all "Englishmen" out of the army, disband the Protestant regiments and replace them with Romam Catholics. In January 1687 the figurehead Clarendon was dismissed and Tyrconnell became Lord Lieutenant. Although it can be argued that James, by means of Tyrconnell, merely effected a return to rule by majority opinion in Ireland, there was much more to the situation than that. To the Scotch-Irish (Scoto-Hibernici) as they now knew themselves, James was that Duke of York who, as Viceroy of Scotland under Charles II, had "amused himself with hearing Covenanters shriek and seeing them writhe while their knees were beaten flat in their boots" (Lord Macauley).

It was well known that Tyrconnell's real intention was to drive all the recent settlers out of Ireland, to destroy the Protestant faith in general, and to restore the old Gaelic hegemony. While many of the Protestants prepared for the inevitable defiance others emigrated to England, where they further enhanced the fears of its Protestant majority as to James's intentions. Following his abolition of the Test Act, James passed two Declarations of Indulgence, the first in 1687, and a fresh one in 1688, whereby toleration was extended to Dissenter and Catholic alike. But to the English Episcopalian of the time the problem was not primarily religious. He feared the political implications of English Catholicism more than its theology; he feared the absolute nature of its claim to represent the ultimate in social order, more than its specific ceremonies; but most of all be began to fear for his country's parliamentary system of government. For, with all his faults, the Englishman had created a form of democracy which has been unequalled in the history of civilization.

As loyalty to James ebbed in England, so the civil power of Catholics increased in Ireland. By the Autumn of 1688 all the judges in Ireland were Catholics as were almost all the highest officers of the State. On 5th November, however, William of Orange landed at Torbay in England with his army, and by the end of the year the King had abdicated and fled to France. There was not, however, a similar constitutional crisis in Ireland where Tyrconnell still held the country firmly for King James. Even in Ulster the Presbyterians "did not at once appear against the king's government". According to J. M. Barkley, "What settled the issue was Tyrconnell's 'sparing neither age nor sex, putting all to the sword without mercy' (to use the words of a survivor) following the Break of Dromore."[2]

Meanwhile the regiment of Lord Mountjoy, which was one of the few essentially Protestant ones left, was ordered to leave Londonderry, which was to be garrisoned by the Catholic MacDonnells under Lord Antrim. Fearing a repetition of the events of 1641, 13 Apprentice Boys of Derry shut its gates against the government troops, a memorable act of defiance by Irish Protestants against a despotic English King. Enniskillen followed suit, and throughout Ulster, defence associations were set up and councils of war elected. On 13th February William and Mary were proclaimed King and Queen of England. On 12th March 1689 James II landed at Kinsale from France and marched north to destroy the latest affront to his authority. On 18th April he commenced the Siege of Londonderry, which lasted a total of 105 days, the longest in British History. During that time one third of the city's 30,000 inhabitants died of injuries, famine and disease. At last, on 28th July, Derry was relieved by the *Mountjoy* and two other vessels. On the day the siege was raised, July 31st, the brave Enniskillens added to their glory the defeat of James's troops under Macarthy at Newtownbutler. News also reached James that the Scottish Highlanders (Jacobites) had been defeated at the Pass of Killiecrankie four days earlier. A fortnight later Schomberg landed at Groomsport, Co. Down, and then marched north to capture Carrickfergus.

Finally, on 14th June 1690, King William himself landed at Carrickfergus and bonfires were lit on all the hills of Antrim and Down (Old Ulidia – Old Ulster). At Loughbrickland in Co. Down the Protestant King reviewed an army composed of Protestants from all over Europe. About half of the 36,000 men were English and the other regiments were from Scotland, Finland, Brandenburg, Holland and Switzerland. Last but not least stood the Huguenots from France with the people of Derry, Enniskillen and the rest of Ulster. All were Protestants except the magnificent unit, the Dutch Blue Guards, who were Catholics. All fought for the love of William, Prince of Orange, King of the Three Kingdoms, at the immortal Battle of the Boyne on 1st July (12th July in modern calendars) when they

The Battle of the Boyne.

decisively defeated James's Irish and French troops. When news reached Pope Alexander VIII of what was for him a French defeat, he ordered torchlight processions in Rome to celebrate King William's victory. The victory was spoiled however by the death of both Schomberg and Walker of Derry in the battle. James fled hotfoot back to France, leaving his Irish general Patrick Sarsfield to defend Limerick, which he did with brilliance. William returned to England, but his army under Ginkel captured Athlone on 1st July, 1691 and defeated the French General St. Ruth and the Irish Catholic forces at Aughrim on July 12th. On 3rd October, 1691, the war finally ended with the surrender of Limerick after a heroic defence, and the "Glorious Revolution" was complete.[3]

The opening of new opportunities for trade, and the cheapness of the land laid waste in Ulster, allowed one last wave of immigration from Scotland during the final ten years of the 17th century. It was estimated by Archbishop Synge 20 years later that about fifty thousand Scots settled in Ulster during this decade. Many were people from the Southern Highlands, members of the Episcopal Church of Scotland and Jacobites. More were to follow after the Jacobite Rebellions of 1715 and 1745. They settled along the North Antrim coast, where the majority now belong to the Church of Ireland and are Gaelic-speaking in origin. From this time on, Ulster was recognised as British and Protestant. The settlement of the Huguenot Louis Crommelin in Lisburn helped in the establishment of a linen industry, which was to set the pattern for its industrial prosperity. The "British" concept was further enhanced in the mainland by the Union of Scotland and England in 1707, a union bitterly resented by many Scottish Highlanders particularly the Jacobites after the notorious Massacre of Glencoe. As for Sarsfield's soldiers, many chose exile and during the next hundred years numerous such "Wild Geese" left Ireland to form the famous Irish brigades of armies throughout Europe.

References

1. Macauley Lord, *The History of England from the Accession of James the Second*, Macmillan (1913).
2. Barkley, J. M. *Francis Mackemie of Ramelton* – The Presbyterian Historical Society of Ireland (Belfast, 1981).
3. During William's reign the National Debt was commenced, the Bank of England established, the modern system of finance introduced, ministerial responsibility recognised, the standing army transferred to the control of parliament, the liberty of the press secured and the British constitution established on a firm basis—Thorne, J. O. and Collocott, T. C., *Chambers Biographical Dictionary* (Cambridge 1984).

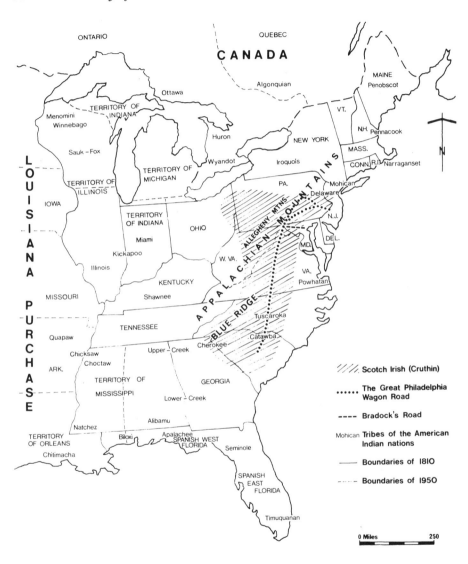

THE UNITED STATES IN 1810 A.D. INDICATING THE EXTENT OF ULSTER SETTLEMENT IN THE 18th CENTURY

CHAPTER 5

The Scotch-Irish

The people of Ulster were to make the greatest of all their migrations in the 18th century, and that was to be a New World. Pressurised by Southern Gaelic expansion into Scotland earlier in the Christian era, they had at last returned to the lands of their ancestors. In every sense of the words they had remained loyal and true. They had maintained the authority of Charles I, had refuted that of Cromwell's Parliamentarians, and had protested against the execution of the King. They had defended Derry and Enniskillen. They had saved Ireland for the British Crown and if Ireland had fallen, so too would Scotland and perhaps even England as well. All this passed for nothing. The English Church was Episcopalian and the "Protestant Ascendancy" which now established itself in Ireland was thus actually an Episcopalian Anglo-Irish one i.e., the "English in Ireland". Having reduced the rebellious Catholics by the harsh Penal Laws under William, which were based on the French Catholic legislation against Protestants, the High Church Party had gained in strength, and by the reign of Queen Anne (1702–1714) were pressing for complete conformity.

In 1704 the Test Act was passed which required all office holders in Ireland to take the sacrament of the Anglican Church. Although ostensibly passed to further discourage Catholicism ,the real object of the Act was to place the Presbyterians on the same plane of impotence. Presbyterian ministers had now no official standing and marriages performed by them were null and void. To the High Churchmen they were actually inferior to Catholic priests, who were considered lawfully ordained in the line of apostolic succession. Presbyterians and other Dissenters could not now serve in the army, the militia, the civil service, the municipal corporations, the teaching profession or the commission of the peace. At Belfast the entire Corporation was expelled, and Londonderry lost ten of its twelve aldermen (Schism Act).

Yet for all that, the Presbyterians had long made their adjustments to religious restrictions, and most bishops of the Church of Ireland were especially tolerant in an age of bigotry. Indeed, Archbishop William King was prominent in his expression of abhorrence to the Archbishop of Canterbury, not only of the risks of increasing alienation of the Presbyterians, but of English commercial avarice in restricting the Irish Woollen trade and the practice of rack-renting by landlords, whereby a farmer's land would be sold to the highest bidder when his lease ran out. The most unkind cut of all was the selling of land in Ulster. One plot of land which had been drained and cultivated by a thrifty "Scotch-Irish" family was sold to two or more Catholic families who could only continue to live there at mere subsistence level. The final straw came with the drought of the 'teen years of the 18th century. This ruined crops, including flax, so that farmers, weavers and townspeople suffered alike. In 1716 sheep were afflicted with the "rot" and many died. Severe frosts ensued and prices soared. Thus began around 1717 the Great Migration from Ulster to America.

One of those Ulster Presbyterians who had previously settled in America was Francis Mackemie (Makemie). Born of Scottish parents near Ramelton, County Donegal, about the year 1657–58, he was enrolled in the University of Glasgow in February 1676 as "Franciscus Makemius Scoto-Hyburnus", and was presented as a student for the ministry to the Presbytery of Laggan by his minister on 28th January 1680. Fleeing from the Jacobite persecution of his day he emigrated to America in 1683, responding to an appeal by a Colonel Stevens. He settled in Eastern Virginia, and in 1706 was one of the most prominent members of the first Presbytery founded in America. Mackemie is justly considered to be the founding father of the Presbyterian Church in America, which was well organised to receive the new Ulster immigrants.

Soon Ulster people were settling in New York State, where they founded the Orange and Ulster counties. The first wave of migration to Pennsylvania (1717–1718) was enough to arouse the English conscience and in 1719 an Act of Parliament was passed to permit Dissenters to celebrate their own form of worship. But rack-renting continued and from 1725 to 1729 there was such an exodus of Ulster Presbyterians to the south-eastern tier of counties in Pennsylvania that their political influence was quickly becoming considerable. That influence was directed increasingly against England. A "feed-back" into Ulster itself helped to make it a centre of radicalism, which was embodied in the establishment of the great newspaper the *"Belfast Newsletter"* in 1737. By 1738 Scotch-Irish settlers had pioneered their way from Pennsylvania into Virginia, of which two modern counties, Augusta and Rockbridge, claim to be the most Scotch-Irish in the present United States. By 1738 their Orange County, with its county seat in the Piedmont, embraced most of the Valley of Virginia, and also much of what is now West Virginia.

The Winter of 1739–40 was known in Ulster as "the time of the black frost", because of the darkness of the ice and the lack of sunshine. This severe weather caused famine all over the island, and a further wave of migration from Ulster (1740–1741). The new arrivals in America now generally went through Pennsylvania down into the Valley of Virginia. Here the McDowell family especially distinguished themselves, and thus did the Ulstermen become the men of Shenandoah. Others crossed the first range of the Alleghenies to settle in the valleys of (present) Highland and Bath counties. From Virginia the line of settlement passed into the Piedmont country of North and South Carolina, and there, as in Virginia and Pennsylvania, German settlements were also effected. Countless German refugees – mostly Protestants – who had crowded into the Palatinate near Holland, had started migrating to Pennsylvania in the late 17th century. William Penn had invited them to live in his colony with the right to practice their faiths unmolested. In addition to Palatinates, Silesians, Alsatians and Moravians also came. The distinctive "Pennsylvania Dutch" art, language and folkways of these German settlers still survive. Expert gunsmiths, the German settlers perfected the frontiersman's long rifle, which the Scotch-Irish were to use with such effect. A third important group were Highland Scots, including the family of Flora MacDonald herself, driven from their homeland following the defeat of Bonnie Prince Charlie (Charles Edward Stuart) at the Battle of Culloden in 1745.

Until the 1750's there had been but sporadic opposition to settlement by the Indians. This was due to the intelligent and peaceful policy of the Pennsylvania Quakers and to the absence of Indian settlements in the Valley of the Shenandoah. There had, however, been revolts by Indian farmers against earlier English settlements, notably Openchancanough's insurrections of 1622 and 1644, the Pequot War of 1637 and Meatcom's (King Philip's) War of 1675–76. In all of these Indian uprisings, the central fact is that native farmers were trying to put a stop to white encroachments and thus restore an earlier and higher status. As Fred A. Shannon has explained, the Indians "were a settled people, living in villages and practising an advanced stage of agricultural economy. They had many hundreds of cleared acres of land on which they grew corn, sometimes a hundred bushels to the acre, in addition to an equal amount of such vegetables as pumpkins, squashes, and beans. For lack of any indigenous animals that could be domesticated for draft purposes, hand implements were the only recourse for cultivation, but for several generations the white man (who looked upon them as savages because of their different complexion and habits) failed to excel these Indians in the quality of produce or the size of crops to the acre."[1]

News of the success of the Scotch-Irish settlements, advertised effectively by the Governors of North Carolina, caused a fresh migration from Ulster during the period 1754–55. From then on, however, the French and Indian War began, and for the next seven years or so the Scotch-Irish frontiersmen were fighting for their lives. Learning quickly from their enemies, they rose to a man against the Indians, and, using similar methods of warfare, carried the war into Indian Territory. Their destruction of the Indians also helped to end the French control of the Ohio Valley. In 1759 Wolfe captured Quebec from Montcalm and by 1760 the British controlled the whole of Canada. By the Treaty of Paris in 1763 France ceded to Great Britain all its American territories east of the Mississippi, which included Canada. This peace was shattered, however, by the Indian Uprising known as Pontiac's Conspiracy.

By this time Ulster's economic situation had improved to such an extent that the vacuum left by the Ulstermen was being replaced by Southern Irish and Scottish Highlanders. In 1771, however, when the leases on the large estate of the Marquis of Donegall expired in Antrim, the rents on the small farmers were so increased that many could not pay them and were subsequently evicted. Resentment had resulted in the formation of secret societies such as the Hearts of Steel, and a final wave of emigration to America from 1771 to 1775. By the end of 1775 at least a quarter of a million Ulstermen had left the Land of the Cruthin during a period of 58 years to form one sixth or more of the total population of the American Colonies. To America they brought a hatred of that aristocratic landlordism exemplified by the Marquis of Donegall. On 20th May 1775 they were the most prominent signatories of the Mecklenburg Declaration of Independence drawn up in Charlotte, North Carolina. They subsequently supported the Declaration of Independence passed by the Continental Congress on 4th July 1776 and they composed the flower and backbone of Washington's army in the Revolutionary War which followed. Their cause was advocated by the *Belfast Newsletter*, and the contemporary Harcourt wrote that "The Presbyterians in the north are in their hearts Americans." The Pennsylvania Line, the famous force of regular troops, was of primarily Ulster descent. George Washington said "If defeated everywhere else I will make my last stand for liberty among the Scotch-Irish of my native Virginia."

For most Ulster people in America as well as in Ireland the most persuasive argument for American Independence was Thomas Paine's *Common Sense*, one of the greatest political pamphlets of all time. One of the most telling passages was the quotation from I Samuel, Chapter 12 to show that monarchy was "ranked in scripture as one of the sins of the Jews." Samuel "set before them their ingratitude, but all would not avail; and seeing them fully bent on their folly, he cried out, 'I will call unto the Lord, and he shall send thunder and rain (which then was a punishment, being in the time of wheat harvest) that ye may perceive and see that your wickedness is great which ye have done in the sight of the Lord, IN ASKING YOU A KING. So Samuel called unto the Lord, and the Lord sent thunder and rain that day, and all the people greatly feared the Lord and Samuel. And all the people said unto Samuel, pray for thy servants unto the Lord thy God that we die not, for WE HAVE ADDED UNTO OUR SINS THIS EVIL. TO ASK A KING.' These portions of scriptures are direct and positive. They admit of no equivocal construction. That the Almighty hath here entered his protest against monarchial government, is true, or the scripture is false. And a man hath good reason to believe that there is as much of king-craft, as priest-craft, in with-holding the scripture from the public in Popish countries. For monarchy in every instance is the Popery of government."[2]

Following the War, emigration slowed and it was as Americans, rather than

Scotch-Irish, that Ulster people joined the advance across the Alleghanies in the fight for the West. Those who did come from Ireland during this period brought their animosities with them and personal violence resulted on more than one occasion. Many persons of the two parties involved, the Ulster "Fardowns" and Southern Irish "Corkonians", engaged in violent encounters at Williamsport in Maryland and at the "high rocks of the Potomac" in the early 1830's. In September 1834 they came to work as labourers on the Wabash and Erie Canal and in July 1835 a serious encounter took place between the two parties which became known in Indiana as the "Irish War". Serious loss of life was prevented only by the intervention of the Indiana militia companies at Wabash, Lagro and Huntington, according to a report issued to Noah Noble, Governor of Indiana by David Burr, one of the canal commissioners.[3]

The American expansion westward was pioneered by Ulster-Irish such as Davy Crockett and Jim Bowie. Sam Houston, also of Ulster descent, organised the rebellion of the Scotch-Irish settlers in Texas against the Mexicans and established the Republic of Texas. The famous Battle of the Alamo, fought in 1836, was viewed by the Texans as a heroic effort in their struggle for independence. Not unnaturally, President Antonio Lopez de Santa Anna of Mexico took a very different view and considered them traitors. The Texas Revolution of 1835–36 resulted from several grievances against Mexico, the most important being the subversion by Santa Anna of the 1824 constitution and his assumption of dictatorial powers. The Texans won the first battle at San Antonio, with the defeat of General Martin Perfecto de Cos on 10th December 1835, but Mexican forces numbering more than 6,000 appeared at San Antonio on 23rd February 1836, and besieged the Alamo, a fortress near the town. The Alamo was defended by a force of 187 Texans, led by William Barrett Travis and including Davy Crockett and Jim Bowie. On 6th March the Mexicans made an overwhelming assault against the post and, on capturing it, killed all of the defenders. Meanwhile on 15th March Texas had declared her independence and Santa Anna's forces were defeated by the main Texas army under Sam Houston in April.

An intriguing narrative of the Alamo, written by the fine Mexican soldier, Vicente Filisola, who was present among the Mexican assailants on 6th March 1836, shows what many Mexicans felt about Santa Anna's judgement at the time:— "Considering the disposition made for attack, our loss should have been still greater if all the cannon in the fort could have been placed on the walls, but the houses inside prevented it, and from their situation they could only fire in front. Furthermore, they had not a sufficient number of gunners. Indeed, artillery cannot be improvised as readily as rebellions. Also our movement from the right and the left upon the north front, and the movement executed by Minon and Morales with their column on the western salient, changing the direction from the southern front as instructed, rendered unavailable the pieces of artillery which the enemy had established on the three other fronts.

Finally, the place remained in the power of the Mexicans and all the defenders were killed. It is a source of deep regret, that after the excitement of the combat many acts of atrocity were allowed which are unworthy of the gallantry and resolution with which this operation had been executed, and stamp it with an indelible stain in the annals of history. These acts were reproved at the time by those who had the sorrow to witness them and subsequently by the whole army, who certainly were not habitually animated by such feelings, and who heard with disgust and horror, as becomes brave and generous Mexicans who feel none but noble and lofty sentiments, of certain facts which I forebear to mention and wish for the honor of the Mexican Republic had never taken place.

In our opinion the blood of our soldiers as well as that of the enemy was shed in vain, for the mere gratification of the inconsiderate, puerile, and guilty vanity of reconquering Bexar by force of arms, and through a bloody contest. As we have said, the defenders of the Alamo were disposed to surrender, upon the sole condition that their lives should be spared. Let us even grant that they were not so disposed – what could the wretches do, being surrounded by 5,000 men, without proper means of resistance, no possibility of retreating, nor any hope of receiving proper and sufficient reinforcements to compel the Mexicans to raise the siege? Had they been supplied with all the resources needed, that weak enclosure could not have withstood for one hour the fire of our twenty pieces of artillery which if properly directed would have crushed it to atoms and levelled down the inner buildings. The massacres of the Alamo, of Goliad, of Refugio, convinced the rebels that no peaceable settlement could be expected, and that they must conquer, or die, or abandon the fruits of ten years of sweat and labor, together with their fondest hopes for the future."[4]

Although the Scotch-Irish were merging quickly now into the American Nation, the Ulster speech itself was to stay alive in the hill-country of Appalachia and beyond, where Scotch-Irish traditional music may still be heard. Among the earliest songs were ballads of King William of Orange, so those who sung them became known as Billy-boys of the hill-country or "hillbillies". Rooted deep in the traditions of the British Isles peasantry, the fiddle had become an instrument of major importance in the development of Irish, Scottish and Welsh jigs, reels and hornpipes. As with folk custom in general, traditional music themes reinforced the ancient cultural divide between North and West Britain and Ireland, and South and East Britain. Transposed to America, the hoe-down fiddle reached the peak of its development in the Southern States. In the latter half of the 1800's came the fiddle-banjo duet and in the early 1900's the fiddle, banjo and guitar trio was formed in the Southern Mountains. Soon, other forms of popular music, such as ragtime and jazz, had their effect on the mountain music. Different styles of fiddling developed, the most important perhaps being that of the Blues fiddling typified by the

Mississippi Sheiks. This style, predominant in the deep South, was one of the richest contributions of the Black people to American life, not only for itself but because of its effect on such Florida fiddlers as Chubby Wise. Playing with Bill Monroe, Wise formulated a new sound which was to become known as Bluegrass.

There are many modern Americans who still take pride in their descent from Ulster-Irish families, though they often know little of Ulster *per se*. Not many of these are now Presbyterians, for most became Methodists and Baptists according to conscience. This was due to old-time preachers whose traditions also lived on in the American Black community to be personified by Martin Luther King. The National Opinion Research Centre at the University of Chicago had indeed introduced statistics which demonstrated that 12% of adult modern Americans named Ireland as the country from which most of their ancestors came and 56% of these belonged to one of the Protestant Churches. Very little about the Ulster contribution to America is taught, however, in our schools and universities. As Harold R. Alexander has written:—"The migration of the Ulster people was a diaspora similar to that of the Jews. North America provided ample scope for the national character and soaring vision of men of Ulster origin . . . It is sad that almost nothing of this is known in Ulster today. English ascendancy and Irish chauvinism have combined to suppress knowledge of Ulster and Ulster-American history, to deny the very concept of the Ulster nation at home or overseas, and to deprive Ulstermen of legitimate pride in their heritage and national identity."[5] Recently, however, the establishment of the Mellon Ulster-American Folk Park at Camphill outside Omagh, Co. Tyrone, had done much to redress the balance.

Deep feelings for their Scotch-Irish ancestors have continued to be expressed in Ulster, notably by W. F. Marshall in *Ulster Sails West* (1943) and more recently by Deirdre Speer in her poem *To America* (1981).

> *Hi! Uncle Sam!*
> *When freedom was denied you,*
> *And Imperial might defied you,*
> *Who was it stood beside you*
> * At Quebec and Brandywine?*
> *And dared retreats and dangers,*
> *Red-coats and Hessian strangers,*
> *In the lean, long-rifled Rangers,*
> *And the Pennsylvania Line!*

Hi! Uncle Sam!
   Wherever there was fighting,
   Or wrong that needed righting,
   An Ulsterman was sighting
      His Kentucky gun with care:
   All the road to Yorktown,
   From Lexington to Yorktown,
   From Valley Forge to Yorktown,
      That Ulsterman was there!

Hi! Uncle Sam!
   Virginia sent her brave men,
   The North paraded grave men,
   That they might not be slave men,
      But ponder this with calm:
   The first to face the Tory
   And the first to lift Old Glory
   Made your war an Ulster story:
      Think it over, Uncle Sam!

W. F. Marshall

To America

Remember me.
My sculpted glens where crystal rivers run,
My purple mountains misty in the sun
My coastlines little changed since time begun,
I gave you birth.

I watched you go.
You saw me fade into the distant sky
You sailed away from me with tear-filled eye,
You said you'd ne'er forget though years passed by,
But time rolled on.

Your young land grew.
And new sons fought to keep their country fair,
And at the Alamo and Shiloh they were there,
And with pride they filled the Presidential chair,
My Ulstermen.

Remember me.
Though battle-scarred and weary I abide
Though Americans their heritage denied,
When you speak of history say my name with pride,
I AM ULSTER

Deirdre Speer

James G. Leyburn's final estimate of Scotch-Irish influence on the formation of the early United States includes the following assessment: "Weber's idea of the Protestant ethic and Tawney's of the connection between Protestantism and the rise of capitalism do not find their most convincing example in the Scotch-Irish; nevertheless, like other Calvinists, they believed in self-reliance, improving their own condition in life, thrift and hard work, the taking of calculated risks. They believed that God would prosper His elect if they, in turn, deserved this material reward by their conscientious effort. Farmers though they generally were, neither they nor their ancestors had been peasants in the sense of blind traditionalism of outlook. Their optimistic self-reliance, with a conviction that God helps those who help themselves, was to become the congenial American folk philosophy of the next century, not far removed from materialism and a faith in progress. The Scotch-Irish were no more the originators of these American convictions that they had been the originators of the idea of freedom and individualism. What is significant is that, holding the attitude they did, and being present in such large numbers throughout most of the United States, they afforded the middle ground that could become typical of the American as he was to become. The Scotch-Irish element could be the common denominator into which Americanism might be resolved."[6] The idea of a messianic destiny which has pervaded American foreign policy owes much to the Scotch-Irish ethos.

References

1. Shannon, Fred A., *American Farmers' Movements*, Anvil Press (Princeton, N.J., 1957).
2. Paine, Thomas, *Common Sense and The Crisis*, Anchor Books (1973).
3. Burr, David, *The Irish War*, Fort Wayne and Allen County Library, Indiana (1953).
4. Filisola, Vicente, in Moquin (ed.). *A Documentary History of the Mexican Americans*, Praeger (1971).
5. Alexander, Harold R., *The Mecklenburg Declaration of Independence*, Ulster Heritage, Glenolden, P.A. (1978).
6. Leyburn, James G., *The Scotch-Irish A Social History*, Chapel Hill – The University of North Carolina Press (1962).

PROCESSION OF BELFAST VOLUNTEERS IN HIGH STREET, 1793.

COUNTY OF } *Adam Millen* ———————— of
DOWN. } *Gordonall* ——————————

In said County, voluntarily made and Subscribed the OATH of Allegiance
as underneath, this **24** Day of JUNE, 1797.

D. Montgomery

I *Adam Millen* ——————————— do
sincerely promise and swear, that I will be faithful
and bear true Allegiance to his Majesty King George
the Third, and that I will faithfully support and
maintain the Laws and Constitutions of this Kingdom, and the Succession to the Throne in his
Majesty's illustrious House. So help me God.

Adam millin

Facsimile of Oath of Allegiance in 1797.

CHAPTER 6

The Year of Liberty

The American Revolution was to have a profound effect on the further history
of Ireland in general, and of Ulster in particular. When France and Spain joined
the Americans in 1778, an invasion of Ireland was feared and an armed Militia
was formed. These volunteers were Protestants, and they quickly became a
political force in the fight for Irish Parliamentary independence. But it was in
Belfast that those heights of radical political philosphy were reached which gave
the town the name of the "Athens of the North". In 1790 the Belfast Volunteers
issued an address to Henry Grattan and Barry Yelverton on the theme of the
independent rights of Ireland. In 1784 the inhabitants of the town pressed for
Parliamentary Reform and the Emancipation of Roman Catholics. In 1789 they
welcomed the French Revolution while in 1791 they celebrated the second
anniversary of the storming of the Bastille and read avidly Thomas Paine's
Rights of Man, written in answer to Burke's *Reflections on the Revolution in
France*.

The natural extension of these sentiments was the invitation of the young
Dublin lawyer Theobald Wolfe Tone to Belfast on 14th October 1791 and the
foundation there of the Society of United Irishmen "to form a brotherhood of
affection among Irishmen of every religious persuasion." Tone had already
recorded in his Diary during his first visit to Ulster in July that Paine's *Rights of
Man* had already become "the Koran of Blefescu", as he nicknamed Belfast in
his private correspondence. In December the proclamation which led to the
famous harper's festival declared that "some inhabitants of Belfast, feeling
themselves interested in everything which relates to the Honour, as well as the
Prosperity of their country, propose to open a subscription which they intend to
apply in attempting to revive and perpetuate the ancient music and poetry of
Ireland." The following year the United Irish Society formed a newspaper, *The
Northern Star*, in Belfast and this was edited by Samuel Neilson, the son of the
Presbyterian minister of Ballyroney, Co. Down. The British Prime Minister,
Pitt, was not completely immune to its pressures, and in 1792 and 1793 Relief
Acts were passed which gave Catholics the right to vote but not the right to
become Members of Parliament.

In 1793 Britain declared War on France, and Pitt pressurised the Irish
government to raise a very largely Catholic militia to defend Ireland for the

49

Crown. The Volunteers were at the same time disbanded by proclamation, and the proprietors of *The Northern Star* prosecuted. The Society of United Irishmen, or Liberty Men as they knew themselves, rapidly became a secret, oathbound movement dedicated to the overthrow of the state. In 1794 a Church of Ireland Clergyman, the Rev. William Jackson landed in Ireland as an agent of the French government, and was captured the following year in possession of a paper which sketched a republican uprising. This paper described the Presbyterians of Ulster as "the most enlightened body of the nation". Jackson was charged with treason and executed in April 1795. Suspicion also fell on Wolfe Tone, who was thus forced to leave for America. Before he did so, he and the Northern Leaders, Tom Neilson, Henry Joy McCracken and Thomas Russell, ascended the Cave Hill outside Belfast, where they swore to overthrow the power of England in Ireland for ever.

But the American War of Independence had also closed the door to further emigration from Ulster for the present, and sectarian rivalry for land began to come into prominence again. In September 1795 following a long period of disturbances Catholic "Defenders" attacked a notorious Protestant "Peep o'Day Boys" tavern at the Diamond in Co. Armagh, and were defeated in a pitched battle. Out of this skirmish was born the Orange Society which was to develop later into the Orange Order. In the Autumn of 1796 a new force named the Yeomanry was enlisted for the government in Ulster, and these were chiefly Orangeman. Yet the majority of the Presbyterians of Ulster remained true to the ideals of the United Irishmen, who had now received a new convert in the tragic young Protestant aristocrat, Lord Edward Fitzgerald. In March 1797 the government decided to disarm the North, and this was done with cruelty by General Lake. Belfast, in particular, suffered the scourge of the Catholic and Gaelic-speaking Monaghan Militia. By May the whole island was put under martial law, and many atrocities were committed both by British Army regiments such as the "Ancient Britons", a Welsh cavalry regiment, and the Orange Yeomen. The latter were not a mass movement at this time but a small, mostly agrarian society who represented the interests of the landed gentry, particularly in Monaghan and Armagh. It is doubtful, however, if United Irish feeling would have remained strong in Ulster if it had not been for the hanging of one of the Presbyterian leaders, William Orr, in September 1797. "Remember Orr" was a slogan as long imprinted on the hearts of Antrim as was "Betsy Gray" later on the Hearts of Down.

The year of 1798 was to be the First Year of Liberty for the United Irishmen. They had now some half-a-million members of whom about one half were armed, and of these 100,000 were Ulstermen and two-thirds of these were Presbyterians. The Rebellion of '98, however, was doomed from the onset. The Northerners realised that they could accomplish little without foreign aid, and this was too slow in coming from the French and their Dutch allies. The almost

Henry Joy McCracken – Commander-in-Chief of the United Army of Ulster.

"American" Presbyterians were increasingly distrustful of France when she quarrelled with the United States early that year. Furthermore, the arrest of most of the Leinster leaders of the United Irishmen in March 1798, followed two months later by their successors, robbed the rebellion of truly United Irish leadership. In particular the arrest of Lord Edward Fitzgerald and the Sheares brothers placed the Leinster forces under Catholic, and often priestly, control.

When hostilities actually broke out on 24th May, it quickly took the character of a religious and bloody war in the south. Only in Ulster, among the Presbyterians of Antrim, Down and East Derry, was the rebellion a truly United Irish one. Even there the Presbyterians were dismayed by the lukewarm support from the Catholics, and finally horrified by the stories of atrocity and massacre of Protestants at Scullabogue on 5th June. On 7th June, however, the United Army of Ulster took Larne and Antrim, but was soon defeated and Henry Joy McCracken captured. On 9th June the Hearts of Down won the Saintfield skirmish and proceeded to Ballynahinch, where on 13th June they were decisively defeated and their leader Henry Monro captured and hanged. His execution was followed by that of the noble Henry Joy McCracken at Belfast on 17th June. Thus did the rebellion in Ulster collapse.

In Wexford there had been more success, but its sectarian nature had little to do with United Irish ideals. The seal of ignominy was set on the Southern movement when 100 Protestant captives were slaughtered indiscriminately at Wexford on 20th June. Paradoxically it was among the loyalist ranks that sectarian animosities were overcome. The Catholics of the militia and yeomanry fought side by side with Orangemen and the force which had contained the rebellion in June was an overwhelmingly Catholic one. Urged on by their leaders, who were of the Protestant Ascendancy class, the Catholic Monaghan Militia were not content with defeating the Liberty Men of Antrim and Down, but burned and pillaged everything in sight, including the entire town of Templepatrick. The *Belfast Newsletter* of 15th June 1798 reported that they had retired laden with booty. By the time the French arrived at Killala Bay, Co. Mayo, in August and at Lough Swilly in September, the rebellion was virtually over. Both these expeditions were defeated and Tone, who was with the latter one, was captured. Rather than be hanged the brave idealist committed an honourable suicide.

A proposed Union between Great Britain and Ireland was seen by the imprisoned United Irish Leaders as actually an achievement of their aims and an admission by the Westminster Parliament that the Irish Parliament had been corrupt and unjust. In 1799 Samuel Neilson wrote from Fort George prison in Scotland:—"I see a Union is determined on between Great Britain and Ireland. I am glad of it. In a commercial point of view, it cannot be injurious; and I can see no injury the country will sustain from it politically." Another '98 leader saw in the Union "the downfall of one of the most corrupt assemblies I believe ever existed, and instead of an empty title, a source of industrious enterprise for the people."

As for the Ulster Protestants, disgusted, dismayed and finally fearful of the new sectarian aspect of "Irish Freedom", many joined the Orange Order, which ironically opposed the Union Act of 1801, fearing Catholic emancipation. The following year one of the '98 leaders, Thomas Addis Emmet, met the First Consul of the French Republic, Napoleon Bonaparte who promised him aid. Article one of Emmet's revolutionary proclamation provided for the confiscation of all church property, an ideal not entirely relished by the Irish Roman Catholic hierarchy. Emmet's brother Robert planned a new rebellion in 1803, but this was poorly organised and ended in debacle. Among those who turned out with the Dublin Lawyer's Yeomanry Corps to hunt down the rebels was a young man named Daniel O'Connell.

The loyalty of Irish Catholics with their Protestant fellow-countrymen to the British concept was fully attested during the Napoleonic Wars which followed. New Regiments, such as the Connaught Rangers, fought like heroes alongside the famous Inniskillings (The Enniskillen Regiment), and it was such men whom Wellington (himself an Irish Protestant) had in mind when he said "It is mainly due to the Irish Catholics that we all owe our proud pre-eminence in the military career." Indeed it has been estimated that at least half the "English Army" under Wellington at Waterloo in 1815 were Irishmen. Certainly, according to Wellington himself, "the 27th of Foot (Inniskillings) saved the centre of my line at Waterloo".

In 1823 Daniel O'Connell formed the Catholic Association, and within six years Catholic Emancipation was achieved. The organisation of a national police administration in the 1830's took power away from the Orange Order. Following an attack on the Order by the great English radical John Hume in 1836 the Grand Lodge formally dissolved itself and its influence declined. In April 1840 O'Connell formed the National Repeal Association backed by the reactionary Archbishop of Tuam. Early support for this also came from the mainly Protestant "Young Ireland" movement, whose ideals were those of '98. Disillusion with Conservative Catholicism came for the Young Irelanders when McHale of Tuam and the bishops insisted that Roman Catholic students at the newly founded Queen's Colleges could not attend lectures in history, logic, anatomy, geology, metaphysics or moral philosophy "without exposing their faith and morals to imminent danger", unless the lecturers were Roman Catholics. Furthermore, O'Connell's call for a "Catholic parliament for a Catholic people" signalled the rebirth of Catholic nationalism, that independent form of Irish Nationalism, alien to the ideals of '98, which brought back memories to Ulster's Protestants of the Rebellion of 1641 and the Massacres of Scullabogue and Wexford. For O'Connell Protestants were "foreign to us since they are of a different religion".

Ulster's
Solemn League and Covenant.

Being convinced in our consciences that Home Rule would be disastrous to the material well-being of Ulster as well as of the whole of Ireland, subversive of our civil and religious freedom, destructive of our citizenship and perilous to the unity of the Empire, we, whose names are under-written, men of Ulster, loyal subjects of His Gracious Majesty King George V., humbly relying on the God whom our fathers in days of stress and trial confidently trusted, do hereby pledge ourselves in solemn Covenant throughout this our time of threatened calamity to stand by one another in defending for ourselves and our children our cherished position of equal citizen-ship in the United Kingdom and in using all means which may be found necessary to defeat the present conspiracy to set up a Home Rule Parliament in Ireland. ¶ And in the event of such a Parliament being forced upon us we further solemnly and mutually pledge ourselves to refuse to recognise its authority. ¶ In sure confidence that God will defend the right we hereto subscribe our names. ¶ And further, we individually declare that we have not already signed this Covenant.

The above was signed by me at‑‑‑‑‑‑‑‑‑‑‑‑‑‑‑‑‑‑‑‑
"Ulster Day," Saturday, 28th September, 1912.

Thomas Lillie

God Save the King.

CHAPTER 7

Home Rule and Rome Rule

At the same time, only in Ulster were the needs of a soaring population met by industrial expansion. The failure of the staple potato crop and the resultant Great Famine of 1845–49, changed the whole political, economic and social history of the island. Massive emigration to America was forced on a starving and disease-ridden population. Many did not get beyond Glasgow and Liverpool. Other emigrants formed in the U.S.A. an unwanted nation within a nation, the Irish-Americans, whose influence on the further history of Ireland was profound.

Following the American Civil War (1861–65), the Irish-Americans formed a recruiting source for the violent anti-British Fenian movement. Founded in 1858 by James Stephens, who had fought in the Young Ireland rising of 1848, the Fenian Brotherhood saw themselves as the inheritors of the ideals of Tone and Davis. Believing that they might provoke an Anglo-American confrontation which would provide an opportune setting for revolt in Ireland, a party of Fenians made a raid on Canada in 1866. This was unsuccessful, as was an Irish uprising in 1867, and further invasions of Canadian territory in 1870 and 1871.

The bravery and tenacity to the ideals of '98 shown by the Young Irelanders and Fenians influenced a former Unionist, Isaac Butt, who had spoken aginst Daniel O'Connell in his youth, to form the Home Government Association. A member of Committee of the Grand Orange Lodge of Ireland, Butt's conservatism was supplemented by a great love of his country. One of the first Ulstermen to join the Home Government Association was John Madden, brother of a prominent Monaghan Orangeman. Madden was disaffected with Episcopalian disestablishment. The Home Government Association gradually grew in acceptability and size so that it became necessary to reconstitute the movement. The Home Rule League was therefore formed in 1873. As Christopher McGimpsey has explained, "This was the turning point and the evolution of Home Government Association to Home Rule League was also the movement away from aspects of Orange Home Rule and Protestant élite nationalism into a more O'Connellite, popular, democratic and Catholic movement."[1] After the election of 1874, Butt was leading a revamped Home Rule Party in the Westminster parliament.

The 1870's and 1880's, however, became known as the Age of Charles

Stewart Parnell, who linked the cause of land reform with that of Home Rule, and moulded the Irish Parliamentary Party into a powerful force. Because of the large Irish Catholic population who had settled in England as a result of the famine, it was now easier for the Fenian Brotherhood (Irish Republican Brotherhood) to gain influence there. In Northern eyes Parnell's association with the Fenians had sinister implications, and this led to a revival of the Orange Order, which became a truly popular movement in Ulster, combining Episcopalians and Presbyterians, Conservatives and Liberals, landlords and tenants, employers and workers, in a fierce opposition to Home Rule. More and more to the Ulster people did Home Rule mean Rome Rule. Prior to the Great Famine, belief in the Elder Faiths had largely survived in rural Ireland. Estimated regular attenders at Catholic communion reached as little as just over 30% of the population. The resurgence of Catholicism following the Great Famine and the unfortunate abandonment of the old Belfast idea of a common Irish identity in favour of O'Connell's Catholic nation convinced many Protestants that Home Rule could only promote the power and influence of the Catholic Church.

Before 1885, there had been a significant liberal element in Ulster politics. The Presbyterians were collateral descendants of the men who emigrated in the 18th century and formed the backbone of Washington's army, and direct descendants of those who joined the United Irishmen of 1798. They had thus carried forward into the 19th century a radical tradition which had become manifested as liberalism. But the crisis brought about by Gladstone's declaration in favour of Home Rule instantly swept all sections of loyalists into one camp. Gladstone had unfortunately been misled by Parnell as to the strength of Ulster feeling on Home Rule. After 1886 the Orange Order expanded to become, in fact, the mass movement of Unionism and the voice of organised Protestantism.

But the real enemy of the British concept in Ireland was not the Roman Catholic Church itself, since the Irish hierarchy actually excommunicated Fenians just as it had excommunicated those Catholics who joined the Liberty Men of '98. A greater threat was the rise of a Gaelic nationalism and its identification with Irish, now essentially Catholic, Nationalism. The finest poet of Ireland in the 19th century was Sir Samuel Ferguson, who was born in Belfast in 1810. Ferguson typified the Ulster intellectual of his day, intensely proud of his "Gaelic" heritage, but without the rancour of the xenophobe. In 1872 he published his masterpiece *Congal* which told of the death of that great Prince of the Cruthin and following his death came the *Lays of the Red Branch*. In fact, the survival today of a large body of Gaelic literature written in Ulster between 1600 and the end of the 19th century was the result mainly of the interest taken in the material by prominent Ulster Protestants, for by the end of the 18th century the guardianship of Gaelic literature in Ulster was taken over by descendants of 17th century settlers such as McAdam, Bryson, Neilson and Reeves.

In 1884, however was formed the Gaelic Athletic Association, which promoted hurling and Gaelic football and forbade the playing of "foreign games". In 1893 the Anglican Douglas Hyde founded the Gaelic League, which had as its aim the "de-Anglicization" of Ireland. From this sprang Gaelic nationalism "Ireland not free only, but Gaelic as well; not Gaelic only, but free as well". Strangely enough, through the Anglo-Irish poets Yeats and Lady Gregory, a pseudo-Celtic Twilight Culture was created, which not only bowdlerised, but Anglicised, the old Gaelic literature out of all recognition. The political manifestation of the "Gaelic Revival" was the foundation of "Sinn Fein" (Ourselves Alone) in 1905. This movement soon attracted and was taken over by the veteran Fenians. At the same time there was a growth of Marxist philosophy, and an active socialist movement was led by James Connolly and Jim Larkin. Connolly however, tried to use Gaelic nationalism to further his own ideals, thus compromising the Labour movement in both Ireland and Britain. The blending of Roman Catholic and "Celtic" mysticism created in people as diverse as Patrick Pearse and James Connolly the myth of the blood sacrifice, which was to have lasting consequences. Confronted by such threats, the British Ulstermen formed an Ulster Unionist Council to fight Home Rule.

Civil War now seemed inevitable. In 1912 the Ulstermen signed a Covenant whereby they swore to use "all means which may be found necessary to defeat the present conspiracy to set up a Home Rule parliament in Ireland". It was obvious that what they really feared was the form of government which was to follow Home Rule. 1913 saw the formation of the Ulster Volunteer Force under Sir Edward Carson and Sir James Craig, the Irish Citizen's Army under James Connolly and the Irish Volunteers under Eoin MacNeill of the Gaelic League. But the outbreak of the Great War in 1914 averted civil hostilities, and Irishmen of all persuasions sailed to Europe to fight for the King and Empire or for the independent rights of small nations. The IRB (Irish Republican Brotherhood) leaders saw this as an opportunity for revolt, and a Republican Uprising was effected without success during Easter 1916. This insurrection and the subsequent execution of its leaders evinced "a terrible beauty" in the eyes of Yeats at a time when thousands of Irishmen were dying unsung in Flanders. On 1st July 1916 the 36th (Ulster) Division sustained 5,500 casualties at the Battle of the Somme, a sacrifice greater by far, as were the losses of the mainly Catholic 16th (Irish) Division at Messines. Nevertheless in 1918 Sinn Fein won a majority of Irish seats at Westminster, and the first self-styled Dail Eireann (Government of Ireland) met in Dublin the following year. There followed a bloody War of Independence fought between the British Irish and the Irish Republican Army, the British Irish being aided by the "Black and Tans", who merely alienated the population.

The British Prime Minister, David Lloyd George, tried a compromise settlement in 1920, which provided for separate parliaments in Northern and

Southern Ireland. Northern Ireland consisted of the whole of Old Ulster (Old Ulidia) i.e. Antrim and Down, as well as four other counties of the contemporary English Provincial configuration of Ulster, which consisted of nine counties. The other 26 counties became the "Irish Free State" in 1922 following an Anglo-Irish Treaty, but the Dominion status of the new State was not acceptable to Republicans. Civil War then erupted between pro and anti-Treaty factions, the former led by Michael Collins, the latter by Eamon de Valera. During the last six months of this war, nearly twice as many Republican prisoners were executed by the authorities of the Free State as were executed by the British in the period from 1916 to 1921. It all ended with government victory in 1923.

In 1926 de Valera formed his Fianna Fail (Warriors of Destiny) Party. The Free State Party (Cumann na nGaedheal) lost power to Fianna Fail in 1933 and changed its name to Fine Gael (Tribe of Gaels) the following year. How many of either party were Gaels in either language, culture or ethnic origins is open to discussion. De Valera's basic Catholic nationalism was highlighted by a radio broadcast on St. Patrick's Day, 1935 when he said "Since the coming of Saint Patrick . . . Ireland has been a Christian and a Catholic nation . . . She remains a Catholic nation." This statement demonstrates, according to Conor Cruise O'Brien, "the peculiar nature of Irish nationalism, as it is actually felt, not as it is rhetorically expressed. The nation is felt to be the Gaelic nation, Catholic by religion. Protestants are welcome to join this nation. If they do, they may or may not retain their religious profession, but they become as it were, Catholic by nationality."[2]

In 1937 de Valera was thus able to produce a new Constitution which was in essence a documentation of contemporary Roman Catholic social theory. Not unnaturally it had its attractions for the Catholics of Northern Ireland, since Craigavon had stood for a "Protestant parliament for a Protestant people". Yet from the onset Carson had pleaded that the Catholic minority should have nothing to fear from the Protestant majority. "Let us take care to win all that is best among those who have been opposed to us in the past. While maintaining intact our own religion let us give the same rights to the religion of our neighbours." That that reconciliation was not achieved was due to faults on both sides. It was particularly unfortunate that Craigavon, one of the greatest of all Ulstermen, who would have wisely accepted Dominion status for Ulster, failed to obtain from the lesser men who were subordinate to him that conciliatory and understanding attitude towards the new Catholic minority in Ulster which was natural to him. It he had done so he would have better served the Protestants of Ulster by leaving them a State fortified with a lasting spirit of tolerance and social justice.

References
1. McGimpsey, Christopher, *Ulster Protestant Nationalism, c. 1690–1900* West Belfast Historical Society, 1982.
2. O'Brien, Conor Cruise, *States of Ireland,* Hutchinson (1972).

Newtownards Road, East Belfast, 1940's showing effects of Nazi bombing near Shipyard complex.

CHAPTER 8

The Troubles

In the early thirties a former commissioner of Police, General Eoin Duffy, became leader of the Southern Irish "Army Comrades Association". This was renamed the National Guard and became known as the fascist "Blueshirts". When the Blueshirts were finally declared illegal O'Duffy became president of the newly created Fine Gael (Tribe of Gaels) Party, but this venture into party politics was not successful. In 1936 he formed an Irish Brigade which fought for Franco in the Spanish Civil War. Left-wing Republican elements as well as Ulster citizens fought on the side of the Spanish Government and for the great libertarian revolution along with Buenaventura Durruti.

During the Second Great War (1939–45) the Irish Free State remained neutral. The Gaelic nationalists had much in common with Fascist Spain but baulked at assisting the German Nazis. Both Britain and the U.S.A. considered the seizure of Southern Irish bases, but Northern Ireland kept the Atlantic lifeline open. Winston Churchill summed this up well when he said, "But for the loyalty of Northern Ireland and its devotion to what had become the cause of 30 Governments or Nations, we should have been confronted with slavery or death and the light which now shines so strongly throughout the world would have been quenched." Following the war, Southern Ireland left the British Commonwealth and a "Republic of Ireland" was formally instituted on Easter Monday 1949. However emigration to England continued on a large scale, so that a substantial proportion of its inhabitants are today of Irish descent. The Irish Nationalist mythos continued to permeate British society, particularly through the Celtic Romantic movement, obscuring from critical analysis one of the most repressive states in Western Europe.

The Republic of Ireland became known by the Gaelic name of "Eire" (from the old Gaelic "Eriu"). Northern Ireland continued to be colloquially called "Ulster" and this usage was also officially established in such Northern Ireland bodies as the Royal Ulster Constabulary and the Ulster Transport Authority. Certainly the State of Northern Ireland had as much right to the name Ulster as had the Province of Ulster. The nine-county Province of Ulster was merely an Elizabethan administrative unit, which has astonishingly achieved sanctity among Gaelic nationalists as the "historic Province of Ulster". In reality it corresponds neither with the old tribal federation of Uladh (Ulidia) which consisted mainly of Antrim and Down, nor with the Gaelic Kingdom of the 14th

61

to 16th centuries. Even if it did, contemporary society is under no obligation to conform to either the British Province or the Gaelic Kingdom. The Earldom of Ulster corresponds more closely to Old Ulidia and this title is still extant in the British Royal Family. Indeed the Earldom of Ulster lies entirely within the territorial configuration of Northern Ireland.

Subsequently in Eire the results of early Irish studies as well as later propaganda were kept within strict political limits. The island of Ireland was still taken as the natural entity and the ancient British or Scottish aspect of its history kept to a bare minimum. This was made easy by the fact that Irish Nationalists were naturally the best Gaelic scholars and thus maintained an anti-British bias. Therefore for 80 years after the formation of the Gaelic League there did not exist a complete textbook of early Irish History[1] and most contemporary historical works remained insular in character. Neither was the British concept fully realised because of the "Little England" mentality of many English historians and the continuing Irish Nationalist sentiment of much of the academic élite. Originating in the 19th century Celtic Romantic movement, the Celtic myth was pursued by writers of popular history and Irish Nationalist political propaganda. The cell structure of academic élitism protected those Celtic scholars who continued to disseminate notions of a Gaelic Aryan Race, to which Ireland rightfully belonged. The extension of similar notions of Nordic man into tools of oppression in Nazi Germany should be an object lesson to those responsible for the education of young persons.

The Protestants who remained in Eire after 1920 were soon to see a reduction in their numbers. No one could be employed in any Civil Service position unless she or he could speak Gaelic. Eire Governmental discriminatory measures included opposition to birth control and divorce and the banning of "anti-Catholic" literature. "Mixed-marriages" regulations which bordered on overt racialism were enforced by the Irish Roman Catholic Church. Dr. Noel Browne's "Mother and Child" scheme of 1951, proposing an element of State subsidisation of health care for pregnant mothers and their children, was opposed by the Irish Roman Catholic hierarchy. Browne was a member of the radical republican party Clann na Poblachta (Republican Family) whose leader, the ex-chief of staff of the I.R.A., Sean MacBride called on him to resign. In the Parliamentary debate following Browne's resignation MacBride spoke for most of the House when he said: "Those of us in the House, who are Catholics are, as such, bound to give obedience to the rulings of our church and our hierarchy." Such sentiments must be considered as a form of religious and cultural imperialism and were an important contributary factor in reducing the substantial Protestant population in the Republic of Ireland by at least one half.

Although Ulster Catholics in general remained in varying degrees antagonistic to Northern Ireland as a political entity, the growing advantages of the British Welfare State led to an ambivalent attitude towards the I.R.A. This resulted in a failure of its campaign against military and police posts from 1956–1962. Feelings of distrust for the Catholic community led Ulster Protestants to believe that the maintainance of a block vote for ultra-unionist politicians was the best defence of their position. The weakness of this stance was highlighted by the formation in 1967 of the N.I. Civil Rights Association, a body which followed trends already in evidence in France and the U.S.A., and to which many Protestants initially gave their support. However, whereas working-class Protestants in similar reduced social circumstances were content to wait until the changes sought by the N.I. Civil Rights Association were made law, Catholics were guided on to a disruptive course by militant elements.

The specific grievances of Catholics towards the Stormont administration concerned discrimination in employment, educational facilities, the control of local councils and housing. However Eileen Evason has emphasised in *Poverty: The Facts in Northern Ireland* that in the case of housing need, for example, the differences between the two communities were less significant that the gap between Northern Ireland and the rest of the U.K. Thus in 1971, while 34.0% of Roman Catholic households lacked a fixed bath or shower 27.6% of Church of Ireland households were in the same position. Taking Presbyterian, Church of Ireland and Methodist households together the percentage without this basic amenity was 25.4%. The figures for England, Scotland and Wales were 8.5%, 12.1% and 13.0%. In other words Ulster Protestant households were twice as badly off as Welsh households. Moreover the gap between Catholic and Protestant was smaller than the gap between Protestant households and the households in the worst-off region in Britain.[2] Finally and very significantly there were, given their greater numbers, as Richard Rose has observed, "more poor Protestants than poor Catholics"[3] in Northern Ireland at this time. The notorious discrimination against Catholics in both central and local government was not a device to further the material interests of the Protestant working class but a political strategy which allowed the Unionist leadership to represent Catholics in general as a continuing threat to the Union, which only Protestant unity could fend off.

In 1911, 63% of the Catholic male work force were engaged in agriculture or as unskilled labourers and 20% of Catholic women were in domestic service. Together they formed a very large and poorly paid group. Under the Stormont system of "majority dictatorship" the Catholic section of the community was able to share fully in the improvement in the jobs available. Indeed by the end of the 1960's, although there remained a marked tendency for Protestants to dominate the upper occupational classes, the higher status industries and the superior positions in work, Catholics in employment had greatly improved their position in Ulster and they compared generally favourably with Catholics in the Republic of Ireland.

In new enterprises such as **the synthetic fibre industry**, in industrial training and in the construction of motorways and large hospitals, Catholics and Protestants were employed without discrimination.[4] Furthermore the higher unemployment rate among the Catholic community must be considered in the light of a higher birth rate, leading to an inevitable trade-off between unemployment and emigration. In the Republic of Ireland an even higher birth rate resulted in even more emigration, much of it to Great Britain, where Eire citizens were still treated as if they were British citizens. Working people throughout the whole island of Ireland were caught in a web of institutionalism and a vicious cycle of poverty which only radical changes in society could obviate.

Nevertheless Ulster Catholic self-perception was, as Paul Arthurs says, that "of a persecuted minority. Every act of the Government therefore could be perceived as an attempt to "do down" the Catholics. It mattered little to them that a majority of their co-religionists lived in peripheral areas where there may have been difficulty in setting up industries. They did not understand that in a scarcity society their unemployment and their larger families made greater demands on the Welfare State."[5] They did not recognise in themselves the twin evils of Gaelic patriotic racialism and Catholic nationalism, which many Protestants felt were threats to the very existence of the Ulster working class. They did not always seem to see that English and "Big House" indifference also affected a large section of the Protestant population. Nor was it important to them that the adjoining counties on the Eire side of the border were among the poorest and most deprived in the Republic. The strategy of Nationalist and Unionist politicians alike had served to convince much of the Catholic community that Northern Ireland was an "Orange State", to which they could never belong.

The original demands of the N.I. Civil Rights Association were actually soon met by the Unionist Government. The Central Housing Authority and the reorganisation of Local Government, begun in 1966 alongside that of Great Britain, removed favouritism in housing and gerrymandering, neither of which were exclusively Unionist customs. As for education, from 1968 the Unionist Government was paying 80% of the capital costing of denominational, largely Catholic, schools, compared with 65% previously. The Catholic community was also benefitted by the transformation of farming under Stormont from a cause of grinding rural poverty into a relatively prosperous industry. Furthermore, whatever the political and social irregularities of a complacent and mediocre Unionist administration the system was served, as John Biggs-Davison has pointed out, "by a Northern Ireland Civil Service of probity and distinction. If the Border was the only election issue, and many Catholics felt themselves 'second-class citizens' much of the blame must fall on those who behaved as if they were not citizens at all and conspired against institutions cherished by the vast majority."[6]

NEWTOWNARDS ROAD, EAST BELFAST, 1970's

The road to the Shipyard complex. Anxious citizens gather to discuss the latest bomb scare.

In 1968 there was a rapid deterioration in the N.I. situation. Friction between those of a more socialist and those of a more nationalist sentiment led to a split in the traditional Republican movement into "Official" and "Provisional" factions. Serious rioting in Londonderry and Belfast in August 1969 opened the way for a deepening of the divisions between the two communities. The sustained efforts of the Provisional I.R.A. transformed the troubles in N.I. into a militant confrontation with the British Army, and relations between the British Army and sections of the Catholic population in the working-class areas became extremely hostile.

In the absence of credible leadership from their elected representatives, groups of working-class Protestants banded themselves together in street defence groups to safeguard their areas, the first being the Woodvale Defence Association. These groups came together in 1971 as the Ulster Defence Association (U.D.A.). Loyalist and unionist suspicions of the real intentions of the British establishment were further aroused when in March 1972 the then British Prime Minister, Edward Heath, announced the suspension of the N.I. Parliament at Stormont and the institution of "direct rule" from Westminster.[7] This was followed by an attempt by the British Government to set up a new administration based on institutionalised "power-sharing" and a "Council of Ireland" which was effectively to form the basis of a future all-Ireland parliament. The Council of Ireland thus made sure that the future of N. Ireland would lie in the hands of English and Eire politicians. This undemocratically constructed "Sunningdale Executive" was brought to an end in May 1974 by a loyalist uprising co-ordinated by the Ulster Workers Council and largely organised by the Ulster Defence Association. The most contentious issue was not, however, power-sharing *per se* but the undemocratic way in which it was applied and the imposed Council of Ireland. In *The Break-Up of Britain* Tom Nairn has concluded that: "It was the working class which made the Ulster nation. Its 1974 general strike defied, and defeated, three bourgeois governments and the British Army. Although they will never concede the fact it relegated the claims of the I.R.A. forever to that historical archive from which they should never have re-emerged. It was without doubt the most successful political action carried out by any European working class since the World War."[8]

Following this period there was an increasing feeling in Ulster that an important section of the British establishment not only felt that a United Ireland was inevitable but actually desirable. Ulster's citizens therefore became increasingly cynical about pledges, talks and conferences on Ulster's future. The basic failure of the British Government in Ulster, as in Cyprus, was their reluctance to promote the common identity of the area they controlled. In his analysis of *The Cyprus Conflict* Zenon Stravinides has written of the British in Cyprus: "Not only was no attempt made to educate the two communities into understanding and collaborating with each other, but two nationalist systems of academic and political education developed, which made it much harder for (the two groups) to communicate and form a basis for political concensus".[9] A similar situation pertained in Northern Ireland. In contrast, working-class loyalists such as Sammy Smyth formulated the concept that the people of Northern Ireland should unite as "Ulidians" to build a better way of life.[10] Whether they were completely aware of it or not, such personalities were touching on a native Ulster tradition of independence which has been disrupted by sectarianism and nationalism since the beginning of the 17th century.

The continuing political thinking going on within the Ulster Defence Association[11] led to the formation in January 1978 of the New Ulster Political Research Group (NUPRG). The terms of reference given to this study group were to develop a constitutional and political framework for presentation to the people of Northern Ireland. The London Times was thus able to report on October 20th, 1978 that the N.U.P.R.G. framework would necessitate a gradual "British" withdrawal and recognition of a new Ulster state by both London and Dublin governments. On the 30th March, 1978, following wideranging discussions in the U.S.A., Europe and Britain, the N.U.P.R.G. published their proposals for a broadly independent Ulster in a document for discussion entitled *Beyond the Religious Divide*. This document suggested a democratic constitutional structure along American lines, with a presidential figure at its head, a Bill of Rights, and a system of sensitive checks and balances for the proper use of power. In their paper on *Some aspects of Nationalism and Socialism in Ireland* (1980), Paul Bew, Peter Gibbon and Henry Patterson included the independent Ulster option along with complete integration as being among proposals which had gained influence "as the likelihood of ultra-unionist or Provisional solutions succeeding has waned."[12] For them the one indisputable democratic gain of the previous ten years was the abolition of the Stormont system and they felt that the current system of direct rule from Westminster was, for all its deficiencies, an improvement on the régime it replaced. Furthermore there could be no solution at the level of constitutional arrangements alone but only a different framework within which the problems would continue to be expressed.

At the same time the Republic of Ireland remained a Conservative Catholic State. On the defeat of his divorce bill in the Eire parliament Noel Browne professed that he "would like to introduce a second motion, that the name of the State be changed to the Irish Holy Roman and Apostolic Republic." Eire's main political parties continued to be called the "Warriors of Destiny" and the "Tribe of Gaels". Speaking at University College, Dublin on 15th October 1980, Breandan O Buachalla complained that "it often seemed, even to a sympathetic observer, that the language 'movement' was merely the cultural wing of Fianna Fail (Warriors of Destiny) and/or the Irish (i.e. Gaelic) speaking branch of the Roman Catholic Church." Furthermore, "The barbaric tearing asunder of Wood Quay

(Viking Settlement in Dublin) was indicative of a certain attitude and mentality of Irish public life which, if unchecked, would make this island the archetypal mid-Atlantic Banana Republic." (author's brackets).

In March 1979 the Assembly of Norwegian Archaeologists had adopted a resolution referring to the importance of Wood Quay for the study of urbanisation in western Europe and to the "catastrophic loss" should the site be destroyed before systematic excavation. Such appeals from serious archaeologists contrasted rather strangely with official Eire assurances to be taken into consideration "particularly the views of archaeologists on site" and with the rather half-hearted position adopted by the National Museum of Ireland responsible for the excavation. Professor F. X. Martin felt that bulldozing at the site had "all the appearance of a last ditch attempt to destroy archaeological evidence."[13] Wood Quay clearly demonstrated to the European Community that in Eire the only culture really thought fit for preservation was Gaelic culture. Annexation by such a narrow and to many "gombeen Free State" was totally unacceptable to the bulk of the Protestant and a significant percentage of the Catholic population of Ulster, whose society was being further enriched by continuing immigration of new citizens, the latest coming from the Commonwealth, including the West Indies, the Indian subcontinent and South-East Asia.

There were several points which still needed clarification to outside observers about Ulster's position within the United Kingdom. Since they were not under conditions of complete integration with Great Britain the loyalty of Ulster people was not to the British Government as such, but to their own traditions under the Monarchy, so long as there remained a mutual agreement between the Monarchy and the people. The Westminster Parliament could not therefore refuse complete integration and simultaneously demand unequivocal acceptance of their terms. If Westminster did not want the Union, then it had no moral right to enforce a United Ireland on the Ulster people. As Craigavon once said "Ulster is nobody's Czechoslovakia". His analogy was that of Czechoslovakia in the 1930's when Nazi Germany used the German Sudeten minority within Czechoslovakia to destroy that country, and the British Government put pressure on the Czechs to concede to the Nazis. Deeply held beliefs that a British Government would actually behave similarly towards a section of its own citizens caused increasing numbers of Ulster people to re-evaluate their constitutional position.[14]

In May 1981 the Ulster Defence Association therefore formed a political party, to act as a pressure group within unionism and founded on the principle that Ulster citizens should be loyal to Ulster first and foremost. Delineating their primary objective as "an Ulster Parliament for an Ulster people", they called for the introduction of an agreed written constitution for Ulster within the United Kingdom and reaffirmed their long-term aspiration as the achievement of Ulster National sovereignty. Reformulating the populist ideals of the Antrim weaver James Hope[15] they felt that an autonomous Ulster T.U.C. should be formed to promote the rights of Ulster workers. They also fully recognised the need to develop a separate Ulster economic strategy. Similar sentiments were subsequently expressed by the former British Prime Minister James Callaghan in a speech to the Westminster House of Commons on 2nd July 1981 when he said that, "Britain should begin a new policy with the ultimate destination of giving the Northern Ireland people complete responsibility for their own affairs." It would take some years, but "the final step would be that the new Northern Ireland would emerge as a broadly independent State."

On 30 May, 1983 Irish bourgeois nationalists set up a "New Ireland Forum". Characteristically its Report was, as Anthony Kenny says, "uneven, ambiguous and not entirely consistent", presenting "a distinctly partisan account of the historical origins of Northern Ireland's troubles".[16] This bias was to be uncritically accepted by the British Prime Minister Margaret Thatcher when she signed a formal agreement with the Eire Premier (Taoiseach) Garret FitzGerald on 15 November, 1985 at Hillsborough Castle, Co Down. The Anglo-Irish Agreement itself was an ingenious document by which the dual objectives of a kind of informal joint authority over Northern Ireland by the British and Eire governments and of administrative devolution within Northern Ireland could be achieved. Lack of consultation with unionists in its formulation and the decision to implement the Agreement by coercion instead of consent were serious errors of judgement by the London and Dublin bureaucrats,[17] and it was regarded as an insult and an outrage by the majority of those most closely affected by it. A more sensitive approach was contained in *Ireland: A Positive Proposal* (London 1985) by Tom Hadden and Kevin Boyle, their thesis being that "difficult conflicts of interest are better resolved by setting out in as much detail as possible the respective rights of the various parties than by leaving them unresolved or attempting to find clever forms of words to paper over the potential differences in the hope that some compromise will be found in the future".[18]

Furthermore the resounding "No" vote by the people of Eire in their 1986 divorce referendum, followed by the affirmation by a Southern Irish politician that non-catholics who had supported divorce were "enemies of the people" continued to demonstrate that unification was not a serious option. At the same time there was evidence of some shift in British public opinion towards an independent Ulster. In January 1987 the N.U.P.R.G. presented a further paper for discussion, named *Common Sense* in honour of Francis Hutcheson.[19] This confirmed the commitment of the Ulster Defence Association to an interim devolved legislative government for Northern Ireland with an agreed written constitution, and suggested, given the suspension of the Anglo-Irish Agreement, a co-operative democratic political structure based on consensus government, proportional representation and shared responsibility. In the words of the

N.U.P.R.G.'s preamble, "It is our firm conviction that the vast majority of both religious communities long for peace, reconciliation and the chance to create a better future for their children. But longing is not enough; there must be a mechanism created to harness the love, generosity, courage and integrity of Ulster people in both religious communities and direct its great power towards the light of a new beginning".

References

1. Byrne, F. J., *Early Irish Kings and High Kings*, Batsford (1973).
2. Evason, Eileen, *Poverty: The Facts in Northern Ireland*, Child Poverty Action Group (London, 1976).
3. Rose, Richard, *Governing Without Consensus*, Faber (1971).
4. O'Leary, Cornelius, "The Political Parties of Northern Ireland", p. 129 in *How Shall I Vote*, ed. Hardiman Scott, Bodley Head (1976).
5. Arthurs, Paul, *Government and Politics of Northern Ireland*, Longman (1980).
6. Biggs-Davision, John, *The Hand is Red*, Johnson (1973).
7. Twenty-four years previously W. F. McCoy, Q.C., had warned of just such a situation developing. Elected at a by-election on April 12, 1945 as a member of the Stormont Parliament for the constituency of South Tyrone, he became Speaker in the Ulster House of Commons before retiring in 1965. In the *Unionist* newsheet of January, 1948 No. 10, Vol. 11 he demonstrated clearly that the Government of Ireland Act, 1920 provided no safeguard for the continued maintenance of Ulster's constitutional position "– if indeed it can be called a 'constitutional position' at all." He therefore advocated dominion status for Ulster, maintaining that "There was one sure safeguard. That was that Ulster should get full and complete independent legislative control over her own territory and destinies." He also revealed that he had "received a message from Mr. de Valera, conveyed to me by the late Mr. Joseph Stewart, M.P. for East Tyrone, that my proposals, if established, would settle the Irish Question." Although the Unionist "Establishment could not be galvanised into activity, or aroused from their slothful, self-satisfied complacency", McCoy continued to support the dominion ideal, writing an account of his proposals in the *Newsletter* of December 31, 1973.
8. Nairn, Tom, *The Break-up of Britain – Crisis and Neo-Nationalism*, New Left Books (1977).
9. Stravinides, Zenon, *The Cyprus Conflict – National Identity and Statehood* (Nicosia, 1975).
10. See also pamphlets *Ulster – A Nation*, Ulster Vanguard, April 1972; *Ulster*, T. E. Utley, April 1972; *Two Irelands or One?* New Ulster Movement, May 1972; *Dominion of Ulster*, Kennedy Lindsay, 1972; *One Island – Two Nations*, The Workers' Association, June 1973.
11. See also Probert, Belinda, *Beyond Orange and Green*, Academy Press (Dublin, 1978).
12. Bew, Paul; Gibbon, Peter; Patterson, Henry, "Some aspects of Nationalism and Socialism in Ireland: 1968–1978" in Morgan and Purdie (eds.) *Ireland* (London, 1980).
13. Martin, F. X., *Irish Times*, 26th May, 1979.
14. Cf., Miller David W., *Queen's Rebels – Ulster Loyalism in Historical Perspective*, Gill and Macmillan (Dublin, 1978).
15. Born in Templepatrick in 1764, James Hope was a hand-loom weaver who taught himself to read and write. He began his political career by joining the Roughfort Volunteers, and in 1795 the Liberty Men. His great ideal was to help create a movement which would restore to the people their natural right – "the right of deriving a subsistence from the soil on which their labour was expended." Between 1795 and 1798 he travelled widely throughout the island organising the working people. A member of the United Army of Ulster he played a leading part in the Battle of Antrim and distinguished himself under difficult circumstances. After the defeat

of the Rising he pursued both his trade and his politics in Dublin, returning to Belfast in 1806. James Hope remained convinced of his ideals until he died at Brown Square, Shankill Road in 1847. His name is commemorated in Hope Street, Sandy Row, Belfast.

16. Kenny, Anthony, *The Road to Hillsborough* (Oxford, 1986).
17. Browne, Noël, *Against the tide* (Dublin, 1986).
18. Hadden, Tom and Boyle, Kevin, "Hopes and Fears for Hillsborough" in *Studies*, No 300, (Dublin, 1986).
19. The great Ulster philosopher, Francis Hutcheson, son of an Armagh Presbyterian minister, was born probably at Drumalig, Saintfield, Co. Down in 1694. He studied for the church at Glasgow (1710–1716) but then started a private academy in Dublin where he was particularly associated with the advanced Presbyterian libertarians, Thomas Drennan, William Bruce and Samuel Haliday. In 1729 he was appointed professor of Moral Philosophy at Glasgow, where he died in 1746. His largest work is *A Sense of Moral Philosophy* (with a Life, 1755). Hutcheson was quite explicit about the right of resistance by the people in the event of a betrayal of trust by a government. He expounded the doctrine of religious toleration and he deeply admired the tradition of armed militias for the protection of civil liberties. The principles he espoused found their way via American revolutionary thinkers into the American Declaration of Independence and are embodied in the American Constitution. Hutcheson's influence on Thomas Jefferson, John Adams and others is discussed in M. White, *The Philosophy of the American Revolution* and G. Wills, *Inventing America* (1980). In fact, Wills concludes that Hutcheson's influence on Jefferson was stronger than that of John Locke. Hutcheson was a pioneer of the "Common Sense" school of philosophy, influenced by Locke; his ethical system is a development of Shaftesbury's "Moral Sense" ethics, in which moral distinctions are in a sense intuited, rather than arrived at by reasoning. See work by T. Fowler (1982) Life by W. R. Scott (1900), and J. Bonar, *Moral Sense* (1930).

THE LANGUAGE OF ULSTER

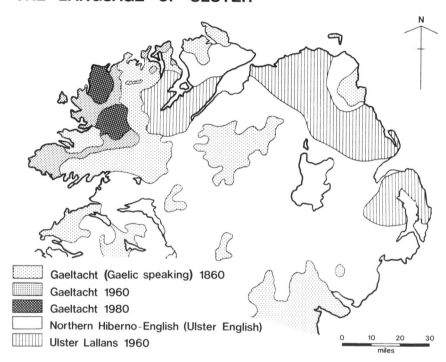

Gaeltacht (Gaelic speaking) 1860
Gaeltacht 1960
Gaeltacht 1980
Northern Hiberno-English (Ulster English)
Ulster Lallans 1960

N

0   10   20   30
miles

CHAPTER 9

The Language of Ulster

Although no literature has survived of the Old British language in Ulster, the Goddodin of Aneirin and the Odes of Taliesin, who wrote in praise of the war-like deeds of his Lord, Urien of Rheged in South-West Scotland, have survived. The oldest Irish Gaelic sagas were composed in a language that suggests that they were first written down in the 7th and 8th centuries from an oral tradition. The most outstanding cycle in the early Irish literature was the Ulster Cycle. The longest tale of this is the *Cattle-Raid of Cooley (Táin Bó Cuailgne)*, dealing with the conflict between "the men of Ulster" and "the men of Ireland" (i.e. the rest of Ireland). The chief hero was Cuchulainn, whose real name was Setanta which is the same as that of an ancient British tribe who have been also recorded as living in present day Lancashire. Old British was displaced in Ireland by Gaelic just as English later displaced Gaelic, so that the Gaelic name Cuchulainn (The Hound of Cullen) is remembered and Setanta became merely his "boyhood name". When Gaelic was planted on the British mainland, however, its verbal system was remoulded on the lines of the old British language, which originally had no future tense. Scottish Gaelic was also to preserve archaic features now lost in Irish Gaelic.

Having worked for more than twenty years on a linguistic atlas of Gaelic dialects, Heinrich Wagner has found that: "each major dialect and each minor subdialect of Gaelic is dependent on its geographical position, all the dialects forming a chain in which two neighbouring dialects always have certain features in common not shared by more distant dialects. The dialect of North Clare, for example, correctly defined as a Munster or southern dialect, has strong features in common with the dialects of South Galway, although Galway Irish on the whole belongs to the central Connaught dialect. The dialects of the old province of Ulster in the north are almost as close to the dialects of Southern Scotland (Arran, Kintyre, and also Rathlin Island) as they are to other Irish dialects."[1]

The earliest extant Scottish document which contained Gaelic matter is the *Book of Deer* in which Latin Gospels were accompanied by marginalia in Gaelic and Latin, the Gaelic being of the 12th century. Many other manuscripts however, of a later date belonged to the common Scots-Irish tradition and the most important of these was the *Book of the Dean of Lismore*, an anthology of verse compiled between 1512 and 1526 by Sir James McGregor in Argyllshire.

This is thought to be the earliest extant antholoogy of heroic Gaelic ballads in either Scotland or Ireland. Later Gaelic prose concerned the hero Finn McCool and his war band, becoming part of the popular tales of the West Highlands and Islands although such stories are as much a part of the heritage of those who returned to Ulster from Galloway and Carrick.

The 1961 census shows that there were still 80,978 Gaelic speakers in Scotland. In addition 3,702 Scottish Gaelic speakers were recorded in the 1961 Canadian census. The survival of Scottish Gaelic is therefore in many ways less in doubt than that of Gaelic in Ireland. This stems from the remarkable fact that the majority of Scottish Gaelic speakers are Protestants, who are accustomed to read the Bible and use it as a vernacular in their religious services. Indeed the first book to be printed in Irish Gaelic was a translation of the Calvinist *Book of Common Order*, commonly called John Knox's Liturgy, published in Edinburgh in 1567 for the use of Presbyterians. Scottish Gaelic was not to become a literary language until the early 17th century.

The division between Ulster Gaelic and that of the rest of Ireland developed well before the arrival of English from the 17th century.[2] T. F. O'Rahilly (1932) outlined a number of features which distinguished the two major Irish Gaelic languages and regarded the position of word stress as one of the most important of these.[3] He believed that the Southern language reached south Co. Meath in the east. The boundary then ran west through Westmeath and Longford to south Galway. The Southern language was more homogenous than that of Ulster and more widespread, occupying at least three-quarters of the island. Ulster Gaelic was characterised by an increasing influence of Scottish Gaelic as one proceeded north and east, though some Scots influence was evident everywhere in Ulster. English was to take over the distribution patterns of the Gaelic language during and after the 17th century, thus perpetuating that ancient frontier between Ulster and the rest of Ireland evidenced also in the structure known as the Black Pig's Dyke.

At the beginning of the 20th century in that area which now constitutes Northern Ireland there were eight districts in which dialects of Ulster Gaelic survived among 5% or more of the total population. As well as the Red Bay Gaeltacht of the Glens of Antrim and Rathlin Island, the Mid-Ulster Gaeltacht centering on the Sperrins lay entirely within what was to become Northern Ireland. There were also three areas along the border which were extensions of localities in which Gaelic was spoken by a higher percentage of people. These were south Armagh Gaelic, which was part of the Old Oriel Gaelic spoken also in Louth and Monaghan, west Tyrone Gaelic which was an extension of Donegal Gaelic, and south-west Fermanagh Gaelic which was an outlier of the Gaelic of Cavan and Leitrim. Perhaps the most literary of these was the Gaelic of Old Oriel. A fourth border area was Strabane, which was formed by immigration from Mid-Ulster and Donegal. The eighth area was around Trillick in southwest Tyrone.

The Gaelic heritage survives in Ulster in place and personal names, e.g. Shankill and Craig. In fact, there are more of these names of Gaelic derivation in Ulster than anywhere else in Ireland. Ulster Gaelic however has seriously declined as a living language. There are now only two small Gaelic-speaking areas in Donegal of 8,400 and 2,000 souls, with a further 15,500 in the remainder of the island (Desmond Fennell). This was due firstly to the effects of the industrial revolution taking people from the land and concentrating them in the major cities which were English-speaking, secondly to the early antagonism of both Church and State and more recently to feelings that Gaelic-speaking had become the weekend sport of the urban élite, with subsequent rejection by the people.

Yet the decline of Ulster Gaelic also owes much to Irish Nationalism itself. The main problem for the early Gaelic nationalist was that there was no single "caint na ndoine" or language of the people to promote as the "Irish Language", but an extensive range of local idioms and grammatical forms. Most scholars agreed with T. F. O'Rahilly that "in the case of Irish it is especially necessary that a standard language be left to evolve itself . . . the pressing problem of the hour is to keep alive and vigorous every one of the few dialects of Irish that have survived. Little good would a manufactured 'literary' language be if once the stream of living Irish . . . is allowed to dry up" (Studies, 1923). In the early 1940's with the development of the Gaelic nationalist urban élite, de Valera requested the translation department of the Eire parliament (since there was no central Academy to direct language reform) to produce a standard reformed spelling. This they did in 1945, followed by a proposed standard grammar in 1953, which was composed mainly of forms selected from Munster and Connaught Gaelic, and largely ignored the Ulster Gaelic of Donegal. This standard grammar has now been generally adopted as the "Irish Grammar". One of the most influential essays prior to its development was *Forbairt na Gaelge* by Niall O Domhnaill, ironically of Donegal Gaeltacht origin. O Domhnaill's work was vigorously nationalistic, strongly advocating the artificial development of a standard language as the "mental tool for a new national life" and he declared that the standard would be created in Dublin. For O Domhnaill the main goal of Gaelic revivalism was "to give Irish a national character". This was bound to engender hostility towards Gaelic among the Unionist population of Ulster, who could have acted to preserve more of their ancient heritage.

The history of the English language starts with the settlement in Britain of Jutes, Saxons and Angles in the 5th and 6th centuries and these population groupings came from respectively Jutland, Schleswig and Halstein. The Jutes settled mainly in Kent, Southern Hampshire and the Isle of Wight, while Saxons occupied the rest of England south of the Thames as well as modern Middlesex and Essex. The Angles, who also settled in what is now modern Friesland in the Netherlands, eventually took the remainder of England as far north as the Firth of Forth, including the area of the future Edinburgh, and the Anglian speaking region developed into two speech groups.

To the north of the river, Northumbrian was spoken and to the south, Southumbrian or Mercian. There were thus four dialects, Northumbrian, Mercian, West Saxon and Kentish. One result of the Norman Conquest of 1066 was the placing of all four old English dialects on a more or less equal level. The Old Northumbrian dialect became divided into Scots and Northern by the end of the 13th century. In its roots and origins Scots was closest perhaps to Frisian and thus is grouped today together with Received Pronunciation or standard English along with Frisian in the language grouping known as Coastal Germanic. This forms with the Dutch and German or Land Germanic the group known as West Germanic. In fact the Anglo-Saxon Boniface was so well understood in Friesland in 754 that it became dangerous for him to stay there. The Frisian heritage is also apparent in the name of Dumfries, which is thought to mean "The Fort of the Frisians."

It must be stated that Received Pronunciation English is not intrinsically superior to other varieties of English but has for purely historical reasons achieved more extensive usage than the others. This may have been fostered by the establishment of public schools such as Winchester, Eton, Harrow and Rugby and its use as the standard English in ancient universities such as Oxford, Cambridge, and Trinity College, Dublin. Irish pronunciation generally has been conservative and is clearer and more easily intelligible than many other dialects. Ulster English in fact preserves many older words than have since gone out of use in England. It has been stated that more of Shakespeare's words are used at the present time in Armagh than in Warwickshire itself. Overall there has been a widespread generalisation of Ulster English (Northern Hiberno-English) throughout Ulster including Belfast. The source of this Ulster language is a mixture of English dialects in the narrower sense and of Lallans. John Braidwood in his classical study *Ulster and Elizabethan English* has pointed out that the English contribution, historical and linguistic, should not be minimized.[4] Brendan Adams (1977) delineated a border between Ulster English and the Southern speech as running between two parallel lines from Bundoran to Dundalk and from Sligo to Drogheda. As with Gaelic, south of a similar line dialects are quite homogenous while north of it Scottish influences have led to more complex regional variations.

There remains however an area in which among the rural population an Ulster Scots language is still spoken. This may be indeed a purer form of Lallans than that spoken in Scotland itself. The language area begins at Whitehead and its borders run south-westwards, approximately a mile distant from the shoreline north of Glengormley down to Dundrod. The line then runs north to the east of Antrim and swings round north of Antrim town to the Long Mountain, progressing then to just south of Rasharkin and then swinging north-west across the Lower Bann nearer Kilrea to continue in a more or less straight line to the shores of Lough Foyle. On the other side of the Belfast Lough it begins at Groomsport running along the Holywood Hills through the Dundonald gap to Gilnahirk and south-westwards through Carryduff and Boardmills to gradually turn round to run eastwards to Strangford Lough, north of Killyleagh. It then commences again at the Saltwater Bridge north of Ardkeen in the Ards Peninsula and runs along this to Cloughey. As well as this large area in Northern Ireland there is the Laggan area of Donegal, the boundary of which begins a mile or two north of Muff and runs across to Lough Swilly then across the Fanad Peninsula through Carrowkeel, Milford, Termon and round to the Foyle near Clonleigh.

From approximately 1770 onwards, Ulster Lallans was cultivated by local poets known as the "Rhyming Weavers", who flourished mainly in Mid Antrim, East Antrim and North Down. Educated in both Latin and Greek, they achieved a higher level of culture than any section of the peasantry in Western Europe. They were not merely writing an imitation of Robert Burns but belonged to a tradition which went back to Allen Ramsey and beyond in Scotland. The greatest period of their activity was roughly the century between 1770 and 1870 but the tradition continues even until today in Co. Antrim. Unfortunately the literature of the people has not been fully developed by the urban élite, although an Ulster Dialect Archive has been established at Cultra Manor, the headquarters of the Ulster Folk Museum.

Brendan Adams exemplified the two different types of Northern speech by reproducing a few lines of the well known poem by W. F. Marshall entitled *Me and Me Da*.[5] Part of the original poem in the Ulster English Language spoken in Co. Tyrone is as follows:

I mind the day she went away,
I hid wan struken hour,
An cursed the wasp from Cullentra
That made me da so sour.
But cryin cures no trouble,
To Bridget I went back
An faced hor for it that night week,
Beside hor own toarf-staack.

Transposed into the Ulster Lallans language of Co. Antrim this reads:

A mine the day she went awaa,
A hud yann strucken oor,
An cursed the waasp fae Cullentraa
Thaat made ma daa sae soor.

But craayin cures nae trabble,
Tae Bradget A went beck
An faced harr for it thaat nagh week,
Beside harr ain turf-steck.

There are many parts of Ulster, therefore, where people are still bilingual in two varieties of the English language. They use Ulster Lallans while speaking among themselves and the approximation of the regional standard of Ulster English, in talking to strangers. (Adams, 1977). Neither Ulster Lallans nor Ulster English are "foreign" since the original dialects were modified in the mouths of the local Gaelic speakers who acquired them and eventually, after a bilingual period, lost their native tongue. These modified dialects were then gradually adopted by the Scottish and English settlers themselves, since the Irish constituted the majority population. The dialect of Belfast is a variety of Ulster English, so that the people of the Shankill Road speak English which is almost a literal translation of Gaelic. In rural areas Ulster Lallans is learned through day by day conversation and communication by a process of natural bilingualism, but is then treated as an inferior dialect by the urban élite. R. J. Gregg has concluded in *Scotch-Irish Urban Speech in Ulster* that local Scotch-Irish urban versions of modified standard English "are spoken nowadays not only by the townsfolk, but by educated country dwellers as well. For this very reason they are obviously destined to expand, for with uninterrupted recession of the rural dialects, the regional modified standard language is spreading out from the towns and rapidly encroaching upon the surrounding countryside."[6]

A similar situation existed for Frisian, the sister language of Lallans. In the 19th century teaching aids for Frisian as a subject were non-existent. In 1907, however, the Provincial Council of Friesland granted subsidies thus enabling the first courses in Frisian for children to be started. These classes, which were run outside normal school hours, did not attract many pupils. In 1924 the Frisian Education Board assumed responsibility for these and other courses and in 1937 it became legally possible for Frisian to be taught as an optional subject. Thanks to the wording of Section 2 of the 1920 Primary Education Act "In those cases where besides Dutch a regional dialect is in active use the subject's reading in Dutch may include some knowledge of that regional dialect." Caution precluded Frisian being mentioned by name but all this was changed by the Amendment to the Act in 1955 when the following sentence was included, "In those cases where besides Dutch the Frisian language or a regional dialect is in active use, the curriculum may stipulate that up to the third school year at most the Frisian language or that regional dialect shall also be used as a language medium in schools." In 1959 the Fryske Akademy established the first educational advisory service in the Netherlands to be fully subsidised by the state. This centre developed a system and paved the way for the production of teaching aids and gave advice to schools which became affiliated to it. In 1974 a further Act of Amendment to the Primary Education Act in Friesland promoted an increase in the use of Frisian as a language medium in all classes. Finally on 1st August, 1980 Frisian was made a compulsory subject. Therefore today while 100% of Frisians are Dutch-speaking, albeit at varying levels, 97% understand Frisian, 83% speak it, 71% speak it at home, 69% can read Frisian, 41% occasionally read a Frisian book, 23% occasionally buy a Frisian book and 31% can write Frisian, 11% well and 20% reasonably well.

In *Policies to support Radio and Television broadcasting in the lesser used languages of the European Community* (New University of Ulster). Antony Alcock and Terence O'Brien summarised the work of the Fryske Akademy as follows: "(a) linguistic research to prepare a course for the teaching of Frisian in primary school, (b) the provision of materials for teachers and pupils, (c) the design of this programme with a view to its use utilising a novel low cost form of telecommunications, i.e. teleboard, (d) follow-up studies to test the results and indicate where improvements might be made."[7] There is therefore much to learn from the Frisian-Dutch Bilingual Primary School system as well as the education system in Wales. There are three types of school in Wales, the first of these is the traditional modern language type of rural Wales, the second Ysgol Gynraeg which originated as a mother language type for small groups of Welsh-speakers in urban areas and the third a bilingual educational project, the Welsh Language School for English-Speaking Children.

The preservation of both Ulster Lallans and Ulster Gaelic must be considered a priority by those who wish to maintain the Ulster identity. Only by the collective will of the Ulster people will either survive. Neither language belongs solely to one or other religious or political "tradition". Both are indeed under threat by the combined influences of British and Irish nationalisms. Ulster should therefore continue to develop as a centre for both conservation and rediffusion. Co. Antrim is particularly well placed with its continuing Lallans literary tradition. The Gaelic of Co. Antrim has fortunately also been completely described by the Swedish dialectologist Nils H. Holmer in 1942, based on fieldwork undertaken in the 'thirties. This East Ulster Gaelic shares features with the Gaelic of Fanad, Glenvar, Urris, and other parts of Donegal as well a that of Western Scotland, where the ancient traditions of Ulster were so long preserved.

The people of Rathlin or "Ragheries" interestingly referred to Rathlin as "an tir seo" or "this country" while the mainland was called "Eirinn" or "Ireland". They were therefore conscious of an older autonomy. Of their language itself Holmer has written: "According to Prof. O'Rahilly (Irish Dialects, p. 191), the dialect is 'essentially a Scottish dialect.' This will, no doubt, be the opinion of any reader who peruses the preceding pages, especially those dealing with the accidence. If it be admitted that this is a characteristic specimen of Gaelic of the

Scottish type, it must not, however, be thought that the difference between the Rathlin dialect and, for instance, that of Kintyre or Arran is approximately the same as between the latter and that of Islay or Skye. Though the distance between Rathlin and the Mull of Kintyre is only about one tenth of the distance between the latter and Skye, the differences are far greater. And, though historically the Rathlin dialect shows closer affinities with Scottish than with Irish Gaelic, the external similarities with the neighbouring Irish dialects are more prominent. This means that a person from Tirconnel would not have very great difficulty in understanding a Rathlin man, while a native speaker from the opposite part of Antrim speaks practically the same language.

The apparent contradiction can be explained in several ways. First of all, the fact that relations with Scotland have been interrupted for over a century must have left its traces in the language. Further, it must be taken into consideration about the Gaelic spoken in opposite parts of Scotland about three hundred years ago (when according to popular tradition the first Scottish settlers arrived) was very different from the present-day dialects of Islay, Kintyre and Arran, and that the Rathlin dialect might be expected to show a number of archaisms. A third very interesting point is whether the Scottish settlers actually came from any of the places mentioned here. There may be some truth in the tradition that the Rathlin people came by the Glens of Antrim. This would mean that the colonization of Rathlin might have been part of the migration westward from Ayrshire and Galloway (which also reached the Isle of Man, cf. O'Rahilly, *Irish Dialects*, p. 117). Some facts which actually point to Ayrshire were mentioned above. In addition, the great difference between the Rathlin dialect and the living Gaelic dialects in Scotland might be more easily explained if it could be assumed that the colonists spoke the Ayrshire dialect of Gaelic, which is now extinct."[8]

Phonetic texts of East Ulster Gaelic have been published in Heinrich Wagner's *Linguistic Atlas and Survey of Irish Dialects* (Dublin 1969) from material selected from 65 texts which he edited as an M.A. thesis, presented at Queen's University, Belfast in 1962. Generous grants towards the work had been made by the Ministry of Education for Northern Ireland and by Queen's University. The source of his texts was the series of recordings made in 1931 by Professor Wilhelm Dogen in East Ulster (including Irishowen, Co. Donegal and Omeath, Co. Louth). Dogen was then Director of the Lautabteilung of the Preussische Staatsbibliothek in Berlin so that copies of his Ulster recordings are now held in both Queen's University, Belfast and at the Institute für Phonetik of the Humboldt University in East Berlin. McAdam's 19th century manuscript dictionary based on Ulster Gaelic is also held for posterity in Queen's University Belfast.

It should prove highly advantageous to the Ulster people that in Working Documents drawn up between 1979 and 1980 the European Parliament,

"Noting that in various regions of Europe movements of ethnic and linguistic minorities are emerging which at times assume forms of frustrated protest and set themselves goals of separation from the national community to which they belong; convinced that such movements reflect legitimate concern for the defences of the heritage, cultural traditions and values which are an integral part of European civilisation," considered that it was time to draw up a Charter of Rights of Ethnic Minorities which within the European context would satisfy the demands for autonomy which inspire such movements and invited the governments to take appropriate action. Only an extension of the educational system with a complete access to all information regarding our language, history and culture will allow the development of that sense of belonging to Ulster which will permit us to cross the religious divide.

References

1. Wagner, Heinrich, *Studies in the origins of the Celts and of early Celtic civilisation* (Belfast – Tübingen, 1971).
2. Barry, M. V. "The Southern Boundaries of Northern Hiberno-English" in *Aspects of English Dialects in Ireland*, The Institute of Irish Studies, The Queen's University of Belfast (1981).
3. O'Rahilly, T. F., *Irish Dialects Past and Present*, Browne and Nolan (1932).
4. Braidwood, John, *Ulster Dialects*, Ulster Folk Museum (1964).
5. Adams, Brendan, *The English Language in Ireland*, (ed.) Diarmaid O'Muirithe, RTE/Mercier (1977).
6. Gregg, R. J., *Ulster Dialects*, Ulster Folk Museum (1964).
7. Alcock, Antony and O'Brien Terence, *Policies to support Radio and Television Broadcasting in the lesser used languages of the European Community*, New University of Ulster (1980).
8. Holmer, Nils M., *The Irish Language in Rathlin Island, Co. Antrim* (Dublin and London, 1942).

BELFAST

(from an original drawing by J. Nixon, published 1793)

High Street, Belfast, about 1820, showing portion of the Old Dock.

CHAPTER 10

A Portrait of the People

EARLY FLAX SPINNING

From an old print

BELFAST, 1864

Queen's Bridge in foreground showing Customs House, Harbour Office, etc., with mountains in background.

BELFAST HARBOUR

From Liverpool boat, showing extent of shipping in the port, both steam and sail.

Welch Collection: Ulster Museum.

OLD NEWTOWNARDS ROAD METHODIST DAY SCHOOL, 1892

This charming class with their teachers shows the work done by churches before the advent of the National Schools. On the left stands Mr. Currie, a much loved and respected schoolmaster and right, the schoolmistress Miss McClelland.

Pepper Hill Steps, Shankill Road, 1894.

Welch Collection: Ulster Museum.

ROPEWORKS, 1910

Here, shown by the camera of Robert Welch, is the Balling Department of the Belfast Ropework Co. Ltd. Note the supervisors (Male) watching the women do the work.   Welch Collection: Ulster Museum.

Again Welch captures the menace of the machine. They almost seem to threaten the women standing before them.   Welch Collection: Ulster Museum.

MOUNTPOTTINGER ROAD CORNER

Somewhere around 1912 with the brand new cinema in the background. Note the Royal Irish Constabulary on duty.   Green Collection: Ulster Folk Museum.

BERESFORD STREET, SHANKILL ROAD

Group of locals posing for the camera. The employment exchange is easily available in the bad times.
Belfast Central Library.

Curing herrings, Ardglass.   Green Collection: Ulster Folk Museum.

Bringing home the "Taties" near Newcastle.   Green Collection: Ulster Folk Museum.

Spinning and winding yarn, Toome, Co. Antrim.   Green Collection: Ulster Folk Museum.

An Irish harvesters dinner, potatoes and buttermilk.   Green Collection: Ulster Folk Museum.

Figure modelling, Belleek Potteries.   Green Collection: Ulster Folk Museum.

Market day in Lisburn, "Let 'em all come".   Green Collection: Ulster Folk Museum.

Riley's Court (Cromac), 1912.   Welch Collection: Ulster Museum.

Raphael Street, 1912.   Welch Collection: Ulster Museum.

Shipquay Place and Old Guns, Londonderry.

Green Collection: Ulster Folk Museum.

*Some of the people who were the back-
bone of the industrial world posing for
family portraits. The background is
Abernethy's Studio in High Street, Belfast.*

*Here, midst the lush forests of the Royal
Studio, Belfast, stands a young man,
with his folded scarf, in lieu of a tie,
holding on to a piece of furniture that he
certainly wouldn't find at home.*

THE SHIPYARD, 1912
*A few of the 15,000 workmen employed by Messrs. Harland and Wolff at Queens Island at this time. In the
background can be seen the ill-fated ship, the Titanic.*

THE GREAT WAR 1914–18

Left: Two of the people involved in this great conflict in which thousands of our young men were wastefully lost. Note the swagger-stick, still in use up to the Second World War. Right: Worker in Dynamite Factory, Isobel Kerr, née Sloan.

ROYAL NAVAL BRIGADE

An unusual group not very well known. Probably used in special circumstances as artillery. It was generally accepted that naval gunners were of excellent quality.

"Oldpark Corinthians" at Oldpark Avenue, 1920's.

Susan Chicken Collection.

26TH TROOP SCOUTS, WINNERS BELFAST SCOUT CUP, 1921–22

Note the names in this group: Corbet, an old English name. McKenzie, whose Irish cousins are McKinney. Mulligan, typically Irish, though sometimes substituted for Molyneux. Carnaghan, properly Kernaghan, meaning–victorious. Magowan at times used instead of Smith – though Smithson would be more accurate, i.e. Mac-Ghabhain, son of the smith. Personal names only indicate male line descent, however. The gene structure of the Ulster people derives mainly from "pre-Celtic" (the author would say Cruthinic) peoples.

Portaferry Charabanc

William Montgomery Collection.

Belfast Water Commissioners "Cart Squad", Royal Avenue.

Neighbourhood frolics – Shankill Road, 1930.

Submitting nomination papers.

Presentation of "Good Luck" Shillelagh. Belfast City Council Election, Shankill Ward, 1946.

Group of election workers with candidate on Election Day.

Victorious candidate with supporters, Belfast City Hall, Belfast City Council, Shankill Ward, 1946.
Susan Chicken Collection.

SIROCCO WORKS

Bearing castings being assembled in the works.

Belfast Central Library.

"CORONATION FLAGS"

Election campaign, North Belfast Constituency, 1950's.   Susan Chicken Collection.

EAST BELFAST

Getting the sun in what little ground that is available. At the top of the hill is busy Dee Street. The trains run close by the end house and on the other side is the Esso plant behind which can be seen the gantries of the shipyard.
Belfast Central Library.

THE BACK YARD, SHANKILL ROAD, 1970's

So typical of the back of a working-class dwelling, many built before the end of the last century (see Pepper-Hill Steps). Most burglars would be pleased to see the ladder on the wall.

Belfast Central Library.

	1889	1890	1891	1892	1893	1894	1895	1896	1897	1898	1899	1900	1901
Dairy & Agricultural Societies	1	1	17	25	30	33	56	61	83	123	153	171	187
Auxiliaries ...							8	9	10	13	38	65	81
Agricultural Societies							10	31	46	77	99	106	106
Co-operative Banks							1	2	3	15	48	76	102
Poultry Societies ...										3	16	21	29
Miscellaneous ...									4	10	18	36	46
Federations ...					1	1	1	1	2	2	2	2	2
Total No. of Societies ...	1	1	17	25	31	34	76	104	148	243	374	477	553
Total Membership ...	50	50	850	1,050	1,250	1,650	3,800	10,120	14,290	27,322	36,583	46,206	51,000

EXPLANATION OF MAP.

Dairy and Agricultural Societies

Auxiliaries

Agricultural Societies

Co-operative Banks

Poultry Societies

Miscellaneous

Federations

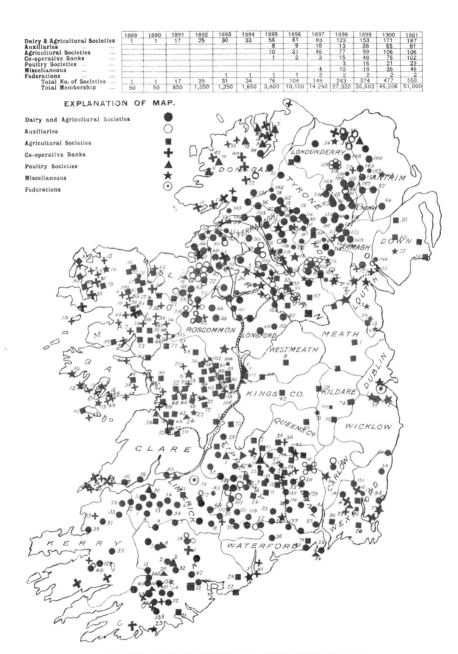

ULSTER AGRICULTURAL CO-OPERATION IN 1902.

CHAPTER 11

The Middle Way

In Northern Ireland during the early 1980's there remained a lower standard of living, a higher proportion of unfit houses, larger families and more unemployment than elsewhere in the United Kingdom. Several groups based on Community Self-Help were finding that co-operative democracy still offered the best chance of making full use of Ulster's resources and creating a classless society. Co-operative democracy is centered on "Co-operation" between bodies of persons for the mutual assistance of both producers and consumers. It thus provides a middle way between capitalism and socialism. The system of Common Ownership is applied, whereby people who earn their living by working in an enterprise own and control that enterprise collectively. Among the first and most successful experiments in co-operation were those of devout Protestant sects who settled in early America e.g. the Dutch Labadists, the German Amish, Mennonites and Dunkers (Church of the Brethren), the Swedish Janssonists and the British Shakers.

The people called Shakers formed a monastic community not unlike those of Early Christian times, with complete equality of race and sex. They knew one another as Believers and used mystic dances and songs as recreations to refresh the spirit following physical labour. Edward Deming Andrews in his classical study writes that "Comparison of the religious behaviour of the Believers with that of other spiritual or primitive sects shows little essential difference in the physical phenomena of worship. The mystical experiences of all spiritual fellowships – the cases of clairvoyance and clairaudience, the speaking in unknown tongues, telepathies, prophecies, and automatisms, all the charismatic gifts associated with the primitive church – were but the signs, as Rufus Jones has suggested, of more important traits 'a unique degree of moral earnestness and passion . . . a rare acuteness of conscience . . . a unique purity of life'." Furthermore, "The Methodists under Wesley and Whitefield and the subjects of the famous Ulster Revival in Ireland exhibited in comparable forms the peculiar psychology attendant on excessive rapture."[1]

For the Shakers manual labour was a sacred commitment, being good for both the individual soul and the collective welfare. As Edward Andrews has written, "The Shaker idea was that in consecration, not compulsion, lay the secret of a successful economy. Age, sex and ability were all considered in

103

assignment to work. But once assigned, the individual became part of a co-operative in which TEMPERATE labor – what one writer called 'the middle way' – was a marked characteristic." Community of goods was most specifically discussed by the prominent Believer of Ulster descent, John Dunlavy, chief minister at Pleasant Hill in Kentucky, who, in *The Manifesto* (1818), treated it under the term "united inheritance". For Dunlavy religious socialism with unity of spirit and possessions was the only logical manifestation of equality and universal love. Only by sharing prosperity with others would such love be genuinely expressed. The fact that individuals widely different in race, age, disposition, education and wealth could form a successful community proved, Dunlavy insisted, that the union was "according to the mind and purpose of Christ himself."

As well as playing an unobtrusive but important part in America's development, the people called Shakers have been justly described as "really the pioneers of modern socialism, whose experiments deserve a great deal more study than all the speculations of the French Schools." Certainly they had a deep influence on socialist theorists such as Robert Owen in England. Historically, with the development of capitalism, control of an enterprise was vested totally in the hands of the "owner". Until just over a century ago the provider of capital was responsible for the success or failure of the venture, taking all the profits or incurring all the losses as the case might be. It was not unreasonable, therefore, that the capitalist would require a measure of control proportionate to the degree of risk involved. The introduction of limited liability in 1855 meant that thenceforth the liability of the investor was limited to the amount of capital that he or she agreed to subscribe to the company. The investor's return, however, remained unlimited, as did the extent of the investor's control. The fundamental injustice of this system led to the formation of the Co-operative movement, the basic principles of which were laid down in 1844 by the Rochdale Pioneers under the influence of Robert Owen. The early co-operators identified a limited return on capital and one person one vote (rather than one share one vote). The Labour movement also embraced the ideal of "common ownership of the means of production". However socialist theoreticians in the Labour movement (particularly Sidney and Beatrice Webb) were opposed to worker's co-operatives in principle, maintaining that "common" ownership would be better achieved by national ownership of the means of production. Hence nationalisation became the Labour Party platform. Therefore the Co-operative movement in Ulster, as in the rest of the British Isles, was left to become mostly consumer. This was the High Street Co-Op, run for the benefit of consumer members and staffed by employees.

Farmers have naturally been in the forefront of the producer Co-operative movement because of feelings that they were at a disadvantage in trading. As early as the 1850's in America Mormon farmers were pooling their labour to irrigate their fields. Founded by Joseph Smith (1805–44) the "Church of Jesus Christ of Latter-Day Saints" was constituted at Fayette, Seneca county, New York on the 6th of April, 1830. Persecution soon followed and the Mormons established eventually the fine city of Nauvoo in Illinois. Joseph Smith's maxim for his followers was that, "We teach them the correct principles and they learn to govern themselves." Co-operation and self-help led to a flourishing community. With the murder of Joseph on the 27th June, 1844, Brigham Young was elected his successor. Fierce persecution continued and the Mormons were forced to leave Nauvoo and its sacred Temple, which was considered to be the most beautiful church in North America. Following "the track of Israel towards the west" the first column of emigrants, including people of Ulster descent, arrived on the banks of the Missouri at the end of June 1846. They passed the winter in the prairies – some in huts, others in tents, and in caves, which they dug in the earth. They underwent dreadful sufferings from cold, want, and disease; many of them perished. Between 1847 and 1868 about 80,000 Mormons emigrated from Missouri to Utah (Deseret as they had wished it to be known), 6,000 died on route. Some travelled with ox teams and some rode on horseback, but hundreds walked – for 4 months – pushing and pulling handcarts and carrying babies in their arms. Yet when Brigham Young died on 29th August 1877 he knew that his people had reached their "Promised Land".

Towards the end of the 19th century a movement in Ireland towards reconciliation, based on social and economic reform was initiated by the progressive Unionist Sir Horace Plunkett. Born in 1854, Plunkett had lived in Wyoming, U.S.A. for health reasons from 1879–89. Returning to Ireland in 1889, he retained a love of America all his life and his sojourn there imbued him with that detached view of Unionism and Nationalism, Protestantism and Catholicism which at times made him one of the least-loved men in Ireland. Widely regarded as the father of the Irish Co-operative movement, Plunkett founded the Irish Agricultural Organisation Society (IOAS) in 1894, with himself as president and the young land-agent, R. A. Anderson as secretary. Two prominent allies were Lord Monteagle in Limerick and Rev. Thomas Finlay, Professor of Moral Philosophy at the Catholic University, who had studied agricultural co-operation in Europe. Then in 1897 Plunkett appointed the Lurgan-born poet, George William Russell (AE) as one of his organisers. Protestant in religion but nationalist in sentiment, Russell's ideal was to "create the conditions in which the spirit of the community grows strong". By the end of 1910 the Co-operative movement had indeed become an important part of the Irish Agricultural scene. The extension of co-operative principles to the whole of society was not effected and producer co-operatives (of which there were hundreds throughout the British Isles at the turn of the century) had dwindled to one or two dozen by the early seventies.

More recently, however, the resilience of modern workers' co-operatives to economic recession has given this most sensible and truly democratic ideal fresh impetus. In 1971 the birth of the Industrial Common Ownership Movement (ICOM) in London signalled a massive growth in new Common Ownership enterprises throughout the U.K. The ICOM identified "model rules" which enabled a group of people who wished to form a Common Ownership enterprise or convert a private firm into a Common Ownership, to incorporate quickly and cheaply. Overall the movement acted as an advisory centre, a federation, a forum, a co-ordinating body and a pressure group. In 1976 the British Industrial Common Ownership Act defined Common Ownership in law. This was unfortunately not applied to Northern Ireland. Nevertheless in June 1978 the Co-operative Development Agency (CDA) was set up by an Act of Parliament, with all party supportl to promote, advise and represent the interests and aspirations of co-operative organisation of all kinds throughout the U.K. It made its first priority the development of industrial and service co-operatives. An important function was the representation of co-operatives' interests to outside bodies, both public and private, to ensure that the two co-operatives would not suffer any undue discrimination because of their structure.

Some of the most outstanding results achieved by co-operative democracy have been in Sweden. Starting with the adoption and use of most of the Rochdale principles from England, discussion group methods akin to those used in Denmark were extended by the Swedish co-operatives who became organised under local and democratic control with an over-all centralized administration. Unity and strength resulted from the Kooperativa Forbundet (KF), which combined both producer and consumer functions and provided educational as well as business facilities. The largest society was the Stockholm Co-operative Society (Konsum). KF acted to keep prices at a fair level where they performed at least 20% of the business in a given commodity. This percentage was found to be adequate enough to protect the consumer without overthrowing the mixed economy. Such co-operatives also remained free from political party allegiances, because their members represented both conservative rural communities as well as the liberal urban élite.

The organisation of the Swedish co-operative system remains a model for all others. The local co-operative societies send delegates to their district congress meetings which in turn elect the National Administrative Council of 30 members. They outline educational and propaganda programs to be implemented during the following season, subject to the action of the National Congress. Thus decentralized control and centralized administration are both obtained. The consumer-producer, the agricultural and the housing co-operative movements are also linked together by co-operation among committees representing each movement. Another model is the complex of industrial co-operatives formed by the Basque People in the north of the Iberian Peninsula.

By contrast the co-operative system in Northern Ireland has been the focus of numerous I.R.A. attacks. The Belfast Co-operative Society now has 40 branches throughout Belfast and their York Street superstore is the largest in Ireland. 1981 brought into existence the Galliagh Co-op of Derry as a model of co-operation and community self-help in an area of high unemployment. The founders of the Galliagh Co-operative movement felt that it would "encourage us to become responsible for our own destiny; developing a social, economic and political consciousness in the whole community, which will enable us to tackle positively the problems that confront us." They looked forward to the time they would be able to graduate from the retail movement to producer co-operatives. If Horace Plunkett and George William Russell had not been hindered by the constitutional problems of Irish politics perhaps such a progressive ideal as this would already have developed in Ulster. For his own part Russell's main criticism of Ulster was that it was not yet itself. He felt that if Ulster was within her own state with freedom to develop her own ideals without looking to English Tories she would be able to express the idealism he knew was there. It was as impossible for Ulster to express herself in the style of English Toryism as it would be for Yeats to express his soul in the style of Milton. Ulster must find herself. She had not yet found her soul because she looked beyond herself, not within herself. His message remains true today. To nurture that sense of belonging and fraternity throughout the whole community by means of our Ulster identity, progressing then to political, economic and social reform.

The modern Ulster person ironically finds himself in a similar positon to the Gaelic apologist MacNeill in his expositions against the Anglo-Irish apologist Orpen, although the positions are now reversed. MacNeill felt that the purpose of his lectures was to correct and supplement those of contemporary historians such as Orpen, for with the best will in the world the picture Orpen painted was bound to be that of an outsider. Similarly today many Eire and English historians have great difficulty in understanding native feeling for Ulster. MacNeill's philosophy was in fact sound when he emphasised the distinction between nationalism and what he preferred to call nationality, and he wrote "I would ask my reader to think again over what is implied in Nicholas Murray Butler's phrase 'the fundamental difference between the nation and the state'. Nationality is to be distinguished from nationalism, which is a political doctrine, meaning localised statism; it is a fact, not a theory; a nation is a species of the genus government. Nationality is the type of civilization which a people had developed, which has become that people's tradition and is distinctive of that people. Nationalities, as such, do not hate each other, do not fear or suspect each other, do not make war upon each other, do not circumvent each other; these being the privileges of statecraft. Neither Europe nor the world suffers any detriment from the diversity of national civilizations. On the contrary, uniformity if it were possible, would be calamitous."[2] Austria (Osterreich or East

Kingdom), for example, is a state whose German nationality resulted in Anschluss by Hitler's Nazi Germany in 1938.

In the expression of his own nationality however, the modern Ulster person has had to leave MacNeill. Though MacNeill was as much an Ulster as he was an Irish nationalist, having been born in the Glens of Antrim, he finally gave his allegiance to a state which included neither the majority of Ulster people nor the Irish cultural province of the Western Isles and Highlands of Scotland, Galloway and Carrick. His insular nationalism ironically ignored this just as effectively as the Anglo-Irish had ignored Gaelic. The modern Ulster person is closer to such figures as the 19th century poet and antiquarian Samuel Ferguson, whose nationality was able to encompass both a British and an Irish sentiment, in which the common denominator was Ulster. Samuel Ferguson felt that history should be developed so that "men may feel that they are not come into the world strangers, but members of a family long planted in the land before them, giving reverence to the place and institutions of their forefathers and by that common sentiment strengthening the social bond among one another".[3]

Again in *Mesgedra* he wrote:

> *"The man aspires*
> *To link his present with his country's past,*
> *And live anew in knowledge of his sires;*
> *No rootless colonist of alien earth,*
> *Proud but of patient lungs and pliant limb,*
> *A stranger in the land that gave him birth,*
> *The land a stranger to itself and him."*

So today we must evolve in Ulster a cultural consensus, irrespective of political conviction, religion or ethnic origin, using a broader perspective of our past to create a deeper sense of belonging to the country of our ancestors. For this Land of the Cruthin is our Homeland and we are her children. We have a right to her name and her nationality. We have a right to belong here, a right to be heard here, a right to be free; free from suspicion, free from violence and free from fear. Let us therefore develop the vision of a new and united Ulster to which all can give their allegiance, so we may achieve a government of all the people, by all the people, for all the people. Only in the complete expression of our Ulster identity lies the basis of that genuine peace, stamped with the hallmarks of justice, goodness and truth, which will end at last the War in Ireland.

References

1. Andrews, Edward Deming, *The People called Shakers*, Dover (1963).
2. Martin, F. X. and Byrne, F. J. (eds.) *Scholar Revolutionary: Eoin Mac Neill*, Irish University Press (1973).
3. Ferguson, Samuel, Lady Ferguson's 1893 edition of *Congal*.

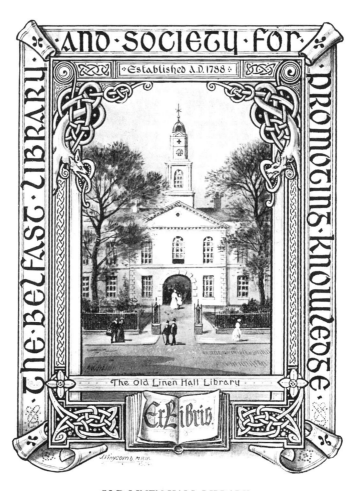

OLD LINEN HALL LIBRARY

The Old White Linen Hall stood on the site now occupied by Belfast City Hall.

(From Book plate designed by J. Vinycomb, 1904).

Bibliography

The best introduction to the history of Ulster lies in the publications of the Public Records Office of Northern Ireland (PRONI). The following collections of documentary material are of abiding interest because of their freedom from polemic.

1–20	*The Great Famine, 1842–52.*
21–40	*Irish Elections, 1750–1832.*
41–60	*The Act of Union.*
61–80	*The United Irishmen.*
81–100	*The '98 Rebellion.*
101–120	*The Penal Laws.*
121–140	*18th Century Ulster Emigration to North America.*
141–160	*The Volunteers, 1778–84.*
161–180	*Plantations in Ulster.*

References

Beckett, J. C., *The Making of Modern Ireland*, Faber and Faber (1966).
Fréchet, René, *Histoire de l'Irlande* (Paris, 1970).
Lyons, F. S. L., *Ireland Since the Famine*, Weidenfeld and Nicolson (1971).
Moody, T. W. and Martin, F. X., *The Course of Irish History*, Mercier (1967).

Belfast Free Public (now Central) Library and Offices of "Evening Telegraph", 1921.

For Further Reading of the native Ulster tradition

The Cruthin, by Ian Adamson, Donard Publishing Co. (1978).
"The Pretanic Background in Britain and Ireland," by Eoin MacNeill, *Journal Royal Society of Antiquaries of Ireland for 1933*, Vol. LXIII, Part I.
The Fir Domnann, by Seamus Pender, M.A., in the same issue.
Lebor Gabala Erenn, Parts I–V, edited and translated by R. A. S. Macalister, Irish Texts Society (completed 1956).
"Táin Bó Cuailgne," from the *Book of Leinster*, edited by Cecile O'Rahilly, Dublin Institute for Advanced Studies (1970).
"Barbarian Europe, from the first farmers to the Celts," by T. G. E. Powell from the *Dawn of Civilisation*, Sunday Times Publications (1961).
An Archeological Survey of County Down, Her Majesty's Stationery Office (Belfast, 1966).
"Ulster," by L. N. W. Flanagan, *Regional Archaeologies Series*, Hienemann Educational Books, Ltd. (London, 1970).
The Ulster Journal of Archeology, U.J.A.
"The Great Wall of Ulidia," *Ulster Journal of Archaeology*, 2nd Series, Vol. III, No. 1, by Rev. H. W. Lett.
"The Peoples of Northern Ireland: An Anthropometric Survey," by Thomas Walmsley, John M. Mogey and David P. Gamble. *U.J.A.* 3rd Series, Volume IX (1946).
"The Dal Fiatach," by Margaret E. Dobbs, *U.J.A.* 3rd Series, Vol. VIII (1945).
"A summary of the Archaeology of Ulster," by Oliver Davies, *U.J.A.*, 3rd Series, Vol. XI (1948).
The Races of Ireland and Scotland, by W. C. Mackenzie, Alexander Gardiner (Paisley, Scotland, 1949).
The Celt, the Roman and the Saxon, by Thomas Wright, Hall Virtue & Co. (1852), including works of Julius Caesar, Tacitus and Ammianus Marcellinus.
The Gael and Cymbri or History of the Irish Scotti, Britons and Gaels, by Sir W. Bethan (Dublin, 1834).
Britain and Ireland in Early Christian Times A.D. 400–800, by Sir Charles Thomas, Thomas & Hudson, Ltd. (1971).
The Picts, by Isabel Henderson and *The Celts*, by T. G. E. Powell.
Ancient Peoples and Places Series, Thames and Hudson, Ltd. (1967).
The Early Christian and Pictish Monuments of Scotland, by Stewart Cruden. Her Majesty's Stationery Office (Edinburgh, 1964).
The Annals of Ulster, Vol. I, A.D. 431–1056, edited and translated by William M. Hennessy. Her Majesty's Stationery Office (Dublin, 1887).
Who are the Scots? Edited by G. Menzies, B.B.C. (London, 1971).
Ireland's Ancient Schools and Scholars. J. Healy, Sealy, Bryers & Walker (Dublin, 1902).
Ireland and the Celtic Church, by George Stokes (London, 1907).
The Irish Tradition, Robin Flower, Oxford University Press (1947).
The Steadfast Man, a life of St. Patrick, by Paul Gallico, Michael Joseph Ltd. (1958).
The Monastery of St. Mochaoi of Nendrum, By H. C. Lawlor, Belfast Natural History and Philosophical Society (1925).
Dromore, an Ulster Diocese, by E. D. Atkinson, W. Tempest, Dundolgan Press (Dundalk, 1925).
Life of Columba, by Adamnan, edited from Reeve's text by J. T. Fowler, Oxford University Press (1894).

A History of the English Church and People, by Bede. Translated by Leo Shirley-Price, Penguin Books (1955).

The Gododdin of Aneirin, translated by Kenneth H. Jackson, Edinburgh University Press (1969).

The Mabinogion, translated by Gwyn Jones and Thomas Jones, Everyman's Library (1949).

The Welsh Triads (Trioedd Ynys Prydain), R. Bromwich (Cardiff, 1961).

The Figure of Arthur, by Richard Barber, Longman (1972).

Sir Gawain and the Green Knight, translated by Brian Stone, Penguin Classics (1959).

Highways and Byways in Galloway and Carrick, by Rev. C. H. Dick, Macmillan & Co., London (1927).

The Story of Galloway, by John F. Robertson, Outram and Co. Ltd. (Castle Douglas, Scotland, 1963).

"The Celts (British and Gael) in Dumfriesshire and Galloway," W. J. Watson, *Transactions of the Dumfriesshire and Galloway Natural History and Antiquarian Society.*

The Imperial Gazetter of Scotland, Edinburgh.

The Ulster Clans, by T. H. Mullin and J. E. Mullan (Belfast, 1966).

A History of the Scottish People 1560–1830, by T. C. Smout, William Collins (1969).

The Ulster Scot, by James Barkley Woodburn (London, 1914).

A Short History of the Church of Ireland, by L. A. Pooler, Olley & Co. (Belfast, 1890).

The History of Ulster, by Ramsey Colles, Gresham Publishing Co. Ltd. (1919).

The Surnames of Ireland, by E. MacLysaght, Irish University Press (1969).

Guide to the library of Bilingualism Centre for Educational Assistance in Friesland, Koen Zondag, Ljouwert/Leeuwarden (1980).

Co-operation in Ireland, Source Document No. 1, T. O'Brien, New University of Ulster (1978).

The Manifesto of Christ, Brian Smeaton, Farset Co-operative Press (1980).

Belfast and the Province of Ulster, W. & G. Baird (Belfast and London, 1909).

History of Belfast, by D. J. Owen, W. & G. Baird (Belfast and London, 1921).

THE BALLYBEEN DOLMEN by DAVID McFERRAN
A symbol of Ulster's Past, Present and Future.

The Setanta Sequence by John Middleton

Cuchulainn, Champion of Ulster, legendary defender of Ulster's boundaries against the "men of Ireland".

Index

117

Trinity College, Dublin, 76
Trotter, R. de Bruce, 12, 17, 31
Turner, James, 27
Tyrone, 74, 77

Ulaid, 5
ULSTER (ULADH, ULIDIA)
—Pre-historic, 1
—Tribal Federation, 3, 61
—Earldom, 62
—Gaelic Kingdom, 10, 61
—Elizabethan Province, 10, 11, 61
—Modern State, 61
Ulster Chronicle, 5
Ulster County, 40
Ulster Cycle, 73
Ulster Defence Association (U.D.A.),
  66–69
Ulster Dialect Archive, 77
Ulster Division, 57
Ulster Folk Museum, 77
Ulster Loyalist Democratic Party, 68
Ulster Revival, 103
Ulster Transport Authority, 61
Ulster Unionist Council, 57
Ulster Vanguard Movement, 69
Ulster Volunteer Force, 57
Ulster Workers Council, 66
Uluti, 1
United Army of Ulster, 52, 70
Urien, 73
Utah, 105
Utley, T. E., 69

Valley Forge, 46
Veigsfjordur, 8
Vikingalo, 8
Vikingr Scotr, 8
Vikings, 8, 68
Virginia, 40, 41
Voyage of Bran, 5

Wabash and Erie Canal, 43
Wabash Militia, 43

Wagner, Heinrich, 3, 16, 73, 80, 81
Walker of Derry, 37
Walsh, 20
Warriors of Destiny Party, 58, 67
Warwickshire, 76
Washington, George, 42
Waterford, 8, 21
Waterloo, Battle of, 53
Webb, Sidney and Beatrice, 104
Weber, 47
Wellington, Duke of, 53
Welsh, 1
Welsh-Speakers, 79
Wentworth, Thomas, 19
Wesley, 103
West Indies, 68
West Saxon, 76
West Virginia, 40
Wexford, 8, 25, 52
Whigs, 23
Whitefield, 103
Whitehead, 76
Whithorn, 5
Wicklow, 8
Wigton Martyrs, 33
Wigtownshire, 20
Winchester, 76
Wild Geese, 37
William III of England, 34
Wilson, Margaret, 33
Wise, Chubby, 45
Wolfe, General, 41
Wood Quay, 67, 68
Woodvale Defence Association, 66
Workers Association, 69

Yeats, W. B., 57, 107
Yelverton, Barry, 49
Yorkshire, 30
Yorktown, 46
Youghal, 25
Young, Brigham, 105
Young Ireland Movement, 53
Ysgol Gynraeg, 79